PRAISE FOR DR. ROLAND HUGHES

I've known Roland and his lovely wife Molly since 1972, so it gave me great joy to see the culmination of his life's work in his book Choices. True to what I know of my dear friend, he combines his decades of personal and professional experience with humor, warmth, and wisdom.

Birdie Yager

Roland Hughes has been a hero, mentor, and presence in my life for over 40 years. It has been an honor to get to know him, learn from him, and now read his book. Roland's words of wisdom are desperately needed in today's world, and once you've read this book, you'll want to get it in the hands of everyone you know! His relational style will draw you in and keep you reading. I cannot recommend this highly enough and am excited to have others share in the wisdom Roland brings us all!

Chad Connelly, *President of Faith Wins*

I've known Roland for many years, associating with him in business. His experiences, life span, intellect, and wit combine for a great book!

Jeff Yager

This is terrific stuff! I started it one evening and sat up late at night because I couldn't put it down. Dr. Hughes' wonderful sense of humor shines through constantly. Lots of practical advice, mixed in with heavy doses of inspiration and marvelous stories. I loved it!

Paul Conn, *Chancellor, Lee University*
Author of The Possible Dream *and* Promises to Keep

Dr. Roland Hughes is my hero!! I met Dr. Hughes about 50 years ago at a seminar he was speaking on entrepreneurship. That one talk he gave was the impetus for me to move forward in life and become successful in the "people business." Since then, I have kept in touch with "Roland," and he has become a lifelong friend of mine. After reading Roland's book, I was struck by his wisdom, which I can attest to personally, and the humor throughout the reading. I have never met anyone nor read a book that can deliver a message like this in one great read.

Angelo Nardone, Jr., *President of Nardone Motivational Enterprises*

Only the best writers can combine information with inspiration, and my dear friend Roland Hughes does just that. Choices is a lifetime of wisdom stuffed into a cornucopia of wit that keeps us laughing while learning. Life is the product of the choices we make. Roland focuses on the top three life choices that lay the foundation for all that follows. This book is a gem. It wraps us in nine decades of insights so wonderfully helpful to anyone seeking to make the right choices.

Hon. Bob McEwen, *US House of Representatives Fmr. Member, Ohio*

Someone once said, "An educator is someone who can take simple information and make it complicated. But a communicator is someone who can take complicated information and make it simple." Although Dr. Roland Hughes has been a college professor in his educational experience, he learned to be a communicator through his business experience. He and Molly are two of my favorite people! I have known them for over 25 years and love them more and more with every interaction we experience. Since Roland took the time to write a book about the power of Choices, you will be well-served by an experienced, educated communicator to read it!

Robert A. Rohm, Ph.D., *President, Personality Insights, Inc.*

CHOICES

*Your Life is the Result of the
Accumulated Choices You Make*

Dr. Roland Hughes

Tremendous Leadership

Tremendous Leadership
PO Box 267 · Boiling Springs, PA 17007
(800) 233 – 2665 · *www.TremendousLeadership.com*

ISBN (paperback) 978-1-949033-79-3

ISBN (ebook) 978-1-949033-80-9

Dedicated to

Roland and Harriet Hughes

The parents who adopted and raised me.

My Aunt Sara Roak

She was always accepting and encouraging of me, the compassionate, giving Mother Theresa of our family.

Sam Riddell

My Scoutmaster who saved my teenage years.

Al Strehle and Ollie Alexander

My two college roommates, special, loyal friends to the end.

Tom Payne, Dexter and Birdie Yager, Jeff, Doyle, and Steve Yager

Friends, leaders, and mentors.

Wendell Estep and Lynn Stewart

Two pastors who inspired and fostered my spiritual journey.

Rich and his son Doug DeVos

Who showed an interest in us, called us by our first names, played tennis with me several times and inspired our career.

Last but not least . . .

Molly my wife, my true love, and my best friend since 1958.

Contents

CHAPTER ONE

Introduction

Impetus

I have written numerous epistles about life to my children and grandchildren, imparting wisdom and encouraging them. I have authored many memos to colleagues as a school administrator and a few articles for national professional periodicals, but never a book. Also, I have given many talks to large audiences all over this country, and in other countries as well, about business practices, attitude, goal setting, relationships, leadership, and overcoming. Over the years, the idea of writing a book occasionally popped briefly into my brain but was soon discarded. An avid reader myself, I have built up a library of more than 3,000 books, and I have respect and admiration for the verbal skills of numerous favorite authors. There are endless possibilities in putting a series of words together. However, writing words and ideas that make sense and are worthy of consumption is a complicated task and a serious responsibility. When thinking about writing a book, I'll paraphrase what the English author Somerset Maugham once said about exercise,

> *Whenever the idea occurs to me, I would immediately lie down and go to sleep until the thought passes.*

One can always come up with good reasons for doing

nothing. My mother used to tell me, "Procrastination is the thief of time." Furthermore, when the elderly look back on their lives, most of them come to an overwhelming conclusion in retrospect: they wish they had been bolder during their lives! Thus, opportunities are missed. Perhaps one reason most people may dodge a daunting new task, like writing a book, is a lack of confidence in tackling a new challenge. As my mentor, Dexter Yager, often said, "Most people overestimate others and underestimate themselves." Dexter was a very successful businessman and entrepreneur, influencing many people globally. While I may have underestimated myself at times in my life, I have rarely overestimated Dexter. If you keep reading, you will see that I have learned immense lessons from many such "Dexterisms."

After several people suggested that I write a book, I began to reconsider the challenge. I had to recognize and accept that I was no longer busy running around in a flurry of activity, accomplishing things in the frantic pursuit of success. At this writing, I am 92. I finally have time to engage in calmer, more sedentary pursuits, such as (why not) writing a book. I feel immortal—so far—and have plenty of time left since I plan to live to be over 100 years old. Actuarial tables clearly show that very few people die over the age of 100!

Maybe you have had thoughts about doing something bold and wavered into abdication. So, as I say to myself at the beginning of this book, let me tell you, "Nothing ventured, nothing gained. Dare to give it your best shot!" I have drawn the courage to proceed based on two motivations: encouragement from family members who love me, and Philippians 4:13, the scripture which says, "I can do all things through Christ who strengthens me." Since I believe God has given me this assignment and helped me through it, success is inevitable.

The Wisdom of the Aged

People often assume that wisdom comes with aging and cumulative life experiences, hence the term the "wise old sage." Unfortunately, this is not always the case. We all know some older neighbors, acquaintances, friends, and relatives to whom aging seems to have come all by itself, without any of the assumed accumulated wisdom. They progressively got older but not necessarily better. We naturally and irrevocably get older, but we must work at getting better consciously. Self-improvement is a lifelong, never-ending process, but more of that later in Chapter IV. These thoughts have become part of my daily prayers, "Lord, help me get better every day, help me become the person you want me to be, and help me know Your will and do Your will."

When reflecting on life, I ask myself if I have been willing to experiment. Have I been open to trying new things, testing my skills, traveling new roads, tasting unusual foods, seeking unlikely relationships, broadening my horizons, and experiencing the spice of life? Just think of how brave the first person must have been to have eaten an oyster!

Some people choose to live out life in a monotonous routine of sameness. Sometimes retired people claim 30 years of experience. However, they did not have 30 years of experience. Instead, they had only had one year of experience 30 times.

What follows in this book, as I write my thoughts at age

92, I like to think of as accumulated wisdom. I hope that you will reflect on what you have read and come to that same conclusion by the time you finish reading this book. I think you will find many gems of wisdom as you consume this book. They are not mine alone, but I have captured them to share and illustrate a point with you. My writing style blends my so-called accumulated wisdom with humorous anecdotes, jokes, and quotations, which in and of themselves are a source of knowledge. However, even though I am a Christian and a conservative, I am not a prude. Some may consider one or two of the stories I have included "naughty," but they are never raunchy, vulgar, crude, or indecent, and there is not a swear word or a dirty word used. Sex is not a dirty word, nor is any part of the human body. Outrageous stories, maybe, but funny. Also, I do not proclaim to have political correctness as a goal. With those stated qualifications, proceed and enjoy!

CHAPTER TWO

Choices Lead to Consequences

hen reflecting on choices in life, it's essential to understand that making choices always leads to something, and that something is referred to as a consequence. And just like choosing leads to consequences, those consequences lead to outcomes. It's a chain reaction. Making choices moves one forward or backward or on a detour, thus establishing direction. Unfortunately, compulsive people don't seem to connect the dots between cause and effect. All potential action first appears as contemplation in our minds before those thoughts are put into action. Bits and Pieces reports that the great steel industrialist Andrew Carnegie once said,

> *Realize that you are responsible for your own choices. Don't ask who is to blame. Ask, what is to be done?"*

Each choice we make leads us onto a particular path. Consequently, our adult lives (independent of heredity or environment) are largely the results of the accumulated choices that we have made, for better or for worse, good, bad, or indifferent. Who you are is a result of heredity and environment. Who you become is the result of the choices you make! We all make good and bad choices during our sojourn. We make errors of commission (what we do which we wish we hadn't done). We make errors of omission (what we don't do that we wish we had done). You will make mistakes!

Proceed with Caution

In our first assembly at (OCS) Officer Candidate School in Fort Sill, our battery commander, Captain Woods, made a statement that has stuck with me. Of course, he was talking about our time during that hot summer of 1952 in Lawton, Oklahoma. Still, his words also applied to the rest of my Army time and to life in general. To the best of my recollection, he told us, "We will watch you like a hawk while here. Our goal is to graduate you as competent into the officer corps of the United States Army. I should tell you that initiative is an important quality for an officer. But I should tell you also to be careful what you choose to initiate. Sometimes it is not always what you do that counts, but what you get caught doing! Remember, everybody makes some mistakes and some bad choices. You can make some small mistakes and small bad choices. But you can't make many BIG ones without dire consequences." Those who did not measure up to Captain Woods' standards would "wash out," a term used in the military when a trainee is eliminated from the program for cause. For us in OCS, as Artillery officer candidates at that time, "washing out" meant immediate transfer, as an enlisted man, to FECOM (Far East Command) or The Korean War in a combat branch.

So, making choices brings consequences. Therefore, the choices we make, and their outcomes, should become learning experiences. Behavioral scientists define learning as a change in behavior. The genius Albert Einstein said, "Insanity is doing the same thing over and over again and expecting different results." We could substitute the word stupidity for insanity and still be correct. If we make a terrible choice and learn from it, we shouldn't continue to make the same mistake again. We should modify our behavior and do something different. We know to make better choices which then bring more positive results. As Dexter often said, "It's not so much what happens to you that counts, as much as how you handle what happens to you."

Confident Choices

We should assume that most people try to make good decisions (I will use decisions interchangeably with the word choices throughout this book). We generally make decisions based on the best information we have available at the time, then go for it, giving the activity our best shot. Once such a decision is made, it is counterproductive to doubt, question our decision, and look back over our shoulders, second-guessing ourselves. Fretting over whether or not we did the right thing only induces worry, anxiety, and confusion that detracts from the achievement of the original goal. Another "Dexterism" is, "Success is just a decision away." This truth implies that the necessary commitment and focus must accompany and follow the determination to succeed. As the saying goes, "Keep your eye on the prize!"

When confronted with making an important decision, I have found one activity very helpful: when in doubt, make a chart. This tool has helped me clarify the pertinent issues and has always led me to a more sensible conclusion. As I think through problems or issues, I list on paper the advantages in one column and the disadvantages in another. I may add to or subtract from my two lists. Sometimes ranking the items in order of importance can help bring clarification. Such a logical progression and analysis never seems to occur with compulsive behavior. Beware!

Let me further suggest a six-step process through which to gain greater confidence in making the right choices, *The Six Cs of Decision Making*:

1. **Confront**. Face up to the issues. Don't procrastinate. Don't dodge the responsibility. List and weigh the alternatives. Eliminate the obvious. Seek a solution. Only a choice on your part will make the confrontation go away and begin the process of metamorphosis into a solution.

2. **Contemplate**. Never rush a significant decision. Take your time. Think about alternative solutions. Weigh the merits and potential outcomes of those different choices. Sleep on it. Mull it over. Pray about it. Seeking the best advice, particularly with essential decisions, begins with going to the Lord in prayer.

3. **Consult**. Seek help. Don't be too proud or too independent to ask for advice. This is where a relationship with a mentor proves to be invaluable. Remember two heads are better than one, especially when one has the smarts, experience, and results that you may not.

4. **Choose**. After gathering related data and facts, it is decision time. As Yogi Berra so wisely said, "When you come to a fork in the road, take it!"

5. **Commit**. Jump in with both feet. Don't hold back.

Go all out to make your choice work out successfully. Don't second guess yourself or look back over your shoulder. It is counterproductive once your decision has been made.

6. **Conclude**. Anybody can start, but personal satisfaction and fulfillment comes to those who see it through and overcome the obstacles. Expect adversity for you to overcome. Nothing worthwhile is ever easy. Stick with it. Show your grit through the grind to reap the glory. See your decision through to a successful conclusion.

Hierarchy

Speaking of rank order, the main idea of this book is to cause you to examine the important choices facing you in life's sojourn and delve further into what I rank as the "Big Three" in importance. Suppose you asked 100 people to rank the significant decisions of their lives. In that case, one might get various items and different orders of significance depending on the rankers' perspective, experience, and considerations. That's OK.

During the writing of this book, I asked several people what they thought were the three most important choices in life. Several, who I knew to be strong Christians, agreed that choosing your Lord is the most crucial choice. Some listed choosing a mate as most important. A few of them listed careers in their top three. Not one person listed improving oneself in the top three. When I revealed my top three, almost all agreed.

I feel confident in my selection of the three most important life choices and have chosen to focus on them in detail. The order in which I have chosen to focus on them is arbitrary, as the order of importance is subject to one's philosophy and how circumstances have impacted each individual differently. You may choose to disagree. No rank order is etched in stone, as each choice is foundational. The reader is free to reorder those in any way desired to fit one's situation. At the very least, my ranking cause you to think about it and form a basis for introspection and discussion.

What is important is to realize that we are the culmination of our choices, and our choices bring consequences in each of these areas. I aim to give you some food for thought in making important decisions.

So, let's proceed to Chapter Three and your third most crucial choice in life, your choice of a spouse.

The 3rd Most Important Choice

Choosing Your Mate

To remain single or get married? That is the question. A wise African proverb states, "If you want to go fast, go alone. If you want to go far, go together." Anyone who thinks marriage is a 50-50 proposition doesn't know the half of it or is bad at math.

If marriage be your choice, the second question becomes, to whom? Because of its lifelong relationship potential, choosing a mate becomes your third most important choice in life! It is one of the biggest earthbound decisions anyone makes. Remember, if you make a wise choice of a mate, you become happy. If you make a wrong choice, at best, you become a philosopher. You are also fortunate if you get this choice right the first time. The heat of youthful passion can too often blur one's normal vision of common sense, resulting in a bad choice for a mate. Before one's passions take over, or the overwhelming desire to settle into married life becomes the consuming objective, think and make sure to get it right.

Two cautions about love and marriage come to us from Hollywood. The captivating and entertaining actress Shirley MacLaine offers this advice for women to consider, "It is useless to hold a person to anything he says when he is in love, drunk, or running for office." Popular actor and director Clint Eastwood shines a different caution on the subject by saying, "They say that marriages are made in heaven. But so is thunder and lightning." For sure, marriage invokes the probabilities of noise, sparks, and fire.

Choose Wisely at the Outset

"Falling in love" is a strange expression and a poor analogy. It should not be an accident like helplessly falling. Think, don't just feel. We make a conscious choice when we decide to love someone. Dexter always has said, "Like happiness and success, love is a decision."

Comedian Red Skelton said, "All men make mistakes, but married men find out about them sooner." Take time to seek advice from family members who know you best and love you most. Making the wrong choice can bring years of emotional grief and financial hardship! Again, do everything in your power to get it right the first time!

Author Michelle Patterson tells the story of a pastor that met with a couple who wanted to marry in his church. When he raised the subject of premarital counseling, the two were quick to reject the idea stating, "We don't need counseling. We've both been married several times before." Quick, raise the red flag! The unteachable gene has just surfaced. I again refer to the Albert Einstein quote, "Insanity is doing the same thing over and over again and expecting different results."

Under our American system of freedom of choice, almost 50 percent of marriages end in divorce or separation. How–

ever, throughout world history, there have been marriages arranged between families and kingdoms to strengthen political alliances or business relationships. A 2019 report released by UN Women entitled "Families in a Changing World" revealed that 55% of marriages across the globe are arranged, and the divorce rate for arranged marriages is a mere 6.3%. These arranged marriages exist in cultures where tradition or respect for parental judgment is more readily accepted than our current western culture would indulge. With such a success rate, perhaps we should throw the process back on mom and dad. Nah!

During the 1920s, my mother worked as a secretary at the University of Pennsylvania (UPenn) in Philadelphia. During that time, my parents befriended a foreign student from Korea named Pum Koo Park who was working his way through medical school at UPenn. Pum's successful and affluent parents made marital arrangements with another family in Korea. That family had a daughter named Kyung Na who was sent over, sight unseen, to be Pum's bride. My parents' relationship with them grew to the point that Pum and Kyung Na were married in their home. A lifelong friendship between our two families grew out of that. Pum became a successful physician at the Crozer Medical Center in Chester, Pennsylvania. Our two families were often together socially which meant that I grew up alongside their two children, Richard and Shirley. The Park family gave their children American names, and they all remained in the U.S. as contributing citizens and as products of a successful arranged marriage. Pum and Kyung Na had learned to love each other; it was a decision.

Opposites Attract, but Compatibility Lasts

A huge factor in the choice of a successful mate is compatibility, which comes from a commonality of background. This means that the more two people have in common, the more they were raised the same way, the more they think alike, the better their chances for a successful marriage. Consider that we "fall in love" with a person's persona. Then in marriage we must live, long term, with another's character. While it is said that opposites attract, remember that similarities endure and coexist more compatibly than differences.

Looks and physical attraction may be the opening criteria upon which to build a relationship, but that is all it is. A traditional Pennsylvania Dutch expression makes a point, "Good looks don't last, good cooking do!" Perhaps you've heard, "The way to a man's heart is through his stomach." I am sure this is what the good-cooking Pennsylvania Dutch had in mind with that expression.

A humorous modern-day variation on that theme alters it a bit to say, "The way to a man's heart is through his stomach . . . or a little lower!" I think it was a famous golf champion who said, "Golf and sex are two things that a man can enjoy even if they're not good at it." Of course, a lasting relationship requires much more than physical, gastronomical, or sexual attraction, granting still the impact and relational contribution of those factors.

At the time of this writing, I am far removed from the flaming passions of youth. The elderly are often concerned about memory loss which commonly afflicts them. One of the solutions offered to ward off memory loss is to regularly take Gingko Biloba pills. I might also suggest that some have found it helpful to take "Gingko Viagra." It helps one remember what sex was like!

Here's a great Milton Berle joke which sheds some light on the joys and sexual habits of the American male:

A psychologist was giving a lecture at a men's club.

"How many of you make love to your wives every night?" he asked. A few raised their hands.

"Twice a week?" More hands.

"Once a month?" Still more.

"Only once a year?" Only one, a man in the back row jumped up and eagerly shouted cheerfully with a smile, "Me!"

"Why do you seem so happy?" the therapist asked.

The man shouted back enthusiastically, "Tonight's the night!"

Honor Your Future Mate

In today's world, pre-marital sex is more prevalent than ever before. Two guys were discussing modern trends on sex and marriage. One said, "I didn't sleep with my wife before we got married, did you?" The other replied, "I don't know. What was her maiden name?"

Someone once asked the question, "Why do they call it premarital sex if one has no intention of getting married?"

Perhaps I should add balance to the subject and offer a sobering truism before you Neanderthals get your hopes too high. Premarital sex is one thing, but cohabiting is the next escalation in the scale of moral promiscuity. Living together before marriage is the next giant step in permissiveness. Regardless, it now seems to be a more accepted, perhaps even an established, alternative practice to the traditional pattern of just dating and only living together after marriage. Since I am writing from the position of a Christian, I'm sure there will be a howl of objections from the non-biblically based people who seem to have a sliding, self-serving, man-made scale of interpreting moral standards.

I know a young man who had been living with his girl-friend for over a year. One day I asked him when he was going to get married. Had they set a date yet? He surprised me by saying that she wasn't the one he expected to marry. I then asked him, "What do you think her expectation is?" He apparently had not thought of that. I suggested that, if marriage was not his intent, he should "fess up" and get out of that arrangement ASAP, which he did, to his credit.

I don't understand why a woman would compromise herself and give up the advantage she has in motivating a man to marry her. It was when I was in the Army that I first heard the expression that pretty well covered the subject of non-commitment, "Why buy a cow when milk is so cheap." Not only does living together take away the mystique and the motivational advantage, but the woman gives up her self-respect and the moral high ground of holding back on principle.

Football great and center for the world champion Green Bay Packers, Bill Curry, had powerful words for this and other important decisions in life. He said, "There are two pains—the pain of discipline and the pain of regret. One is temporary. The other lasts forever. You alone decide which to endure." Isn't that the unbridled truth?

Research even shows a long-term detriment to living together before marriage. In What are the Chances, Siskin, Staller, and Rorvik reported findings on this practice. When asked, "Do marriages last longer if the couple lives together first?" The answer was a resounding, "No." They said, "A recent study suggests that couples who live together are over 33% more likely to divorce. Unmarried couples who cohabit seem not to feel as 'bound' by their vows later on." Despite the fact that couples living together seems to be more prevalent and accepted in recent years, research continues to suggest that cohabitation does not lead to more successful marriages.

In his book, *Calling the Called*, author and businessman Dennis Delisle cites a Penn State study which indicates important findings:

1. Married couples who cohabitated before marriage showed poorer communications skills than those who didn't.

2. Cohabiters have a higher incidence of violence and abuse than married people.

3. The National Institute of Mental Health found that women in cohabiting relationships had rates of depression five times higher than married women.

4. The National Sex Survey reports that cohabiting men are nearly four times more likely than husbands to cheat on their partner, and cohabiting women are eight times more likely than wives to cheat.

I might as well add that wives would do well to know and remember that we males are straightforward creatures with a small number of simple, basic needs. In our passionate youth, we anticipated (in our imagined dreams of marital bliss) that our wife-to-be would meet those simple basic needs by always bringing food and arriving naked.

A national poll conducted a decade ago highlights the basic differences in the way men and women think. Sex ranked number one in importance with male respondents. With women, however, sex ranked number thirteen in importance right after number twelve, gardening. I bet that lets some air out of your tires. Nah, it just reflects and confirms the challenge we men have always faced with the different perspective of the opposite sex. More than one frazzled wife and mother of several little ones at home preparing supper has said to her romantically motivated husband as he ardently embraced her, "Why can't you come home from work exhausted like other men?" See what I mean?

Innate Differences

As the French have said all along, *"Vive La Difference!"* We rejoice in differences, and those differences lead to some humorous anecdotes. Simple mannerisms often distinguish male from female as indicated in the following story.

A wife came home to find her husband stalking with a fly swatter in his hand. She asked playfully, "Kill any?"

"Yep," he responded, "two males and one female."

"They're only flies. How could you tell?"

He said, "Easy. Two were on a beer can and one was on the phone."

I heard one story about the differences between men and

women that occurred in a university course. The professor apparently divided the class between men and women and issued the assignment. Each team was given the challenge to determine the gender of the computer. Then they were to give reasons to substantiate their choice. The two groups rose to the challenge. They discussed, brainstormed, and debated at length. Then each team came up with their answer to the question and were ready to give their reasons.

The men went first and said the computer was definitely female and gave four reasons for their decision:

1. No one but their creator can understand their internal logic.
2. When computers communicate with one another, they speak in a code that only they and experts can understand.
3. Every mistake you make is stored in their hard drive for later retrieval.
4. As soon as you commit to one, you have to spend a good chunk of your money accessorizing them.

Then it was the woman's turn. They firmly said that, without a doubt, the computer was of the male gender. They too gave four reasons to substantiate their claim:

1. In order to get their attention, you first have to turn them on.
2. They have a lot of data but still can't think for themselves.
3. They are supposed to help you solve problems, but too often, they are the problem.
4. As soon as you commit to one, you realize that if you had waited a little longer, you could have

gotten a better model.

There are obvious and subtle differences between men and women that are too numerous to mention. However, there are many who facetiously would agree that, in general, a woman worries about her future until she gets a husband, whereas a man never really worries about his future until he gets a wife.

Here is another example to make you smile. To women, shopping is both a practical exercise and a leisure activity, to be enjoyed and savored. If men want to buy something, they know what store has it and on which aisle to find it. They make a beeline for it, spend as little time as possible purchasing it, then exit the store by the nearest door and are on to other pursuits. Furthermore, a man will pay $2.00 for a $1.00 item he needs, whereas, a woman will pay $1.00 for a $2.00 item she doesn't need.

The best example I've heard regarding the difference in men's and women's attitude towards shopping came to me in an e-mail. It concerns shopping at "The Husband Store" and then at "The Wife Store." A new store opened for women to be able to select a husband. A woman could choose any item on any floor of the store. Instructions posted at the entrance read:

You may visit the store only once. The store has six floors. As you go up, you cannot go back down. You may select from the floor you are on or go on to the next higher floor. Remember, you cannot go back down, and this is your only visit to The Husband Store. As you advance to a higher floor, the products increase in value. OK, begin!

· 1st Floor – All potential husbands have jobs.

- 2nd Floor – All potential husbands have jobs and love kids.
- 3rd Floor – All potential husbands have jobs, love kids, and are really good looking.
- 4th Floor – All potential husbands have high paying jobs, love kids, are drop dead gorgeous and help with the housework.
- 5th Floor – All potential husbands have high paying jobs, love kids, are drop dead gorgeous, help with the housework, and have a strong romantic streak.
- 6th Floor – You are the 31,536th visitor to this floor. There are no men here. This floor exists only to prove that women are never satisfied. Thank you for shopping at The Husband Store. Please exit now.

The Husband Store was so successful that it was decided to open The Wives Store across the street. Same rules apply.

- 1st Floor – All potential wives on this floor are lovers and sexy.
- 2nd Floor – All potential wives on this floor are lovers and sexy, as well as beautiful and sweet.
- 3rd Floor – All potential wives on this floor are lovers and sexy, beautiful and sweet, and have money.
- The 4th, 5th, and 6th Floors have never been visited!

The Verbally Gifted

God has given women a larger quota of words than men to use each day. Women like to talk and to have someone listen to them. My friend and business associate, Jerry Meadows, has said, "When your wife comes to you wanting to discuss problems, she just needs you to listen to her." A different story tells of a son who noticed that his 70-year-old father was losing his hearing. He mentioned this concern to his mother. The mother replied, "Don't worry about it, my boy. Things haven't really changed much. Before, your dad didn't listen, and now he can't hear."

Often men are accused of being poor listeners. Partially that is true, in part because women give us so many more words than are needed. We men don't need a lengthy explanation or lecture. Just give us the facts. Sometimes just OK, yes, or no will do. Keep it simple, eh? I wonder if any other men experience what I have experienced many times with my wife Molly. Not only do women appear to use more words than necessary, but they also seem to speak in the oblique.

For example, the Friday before Thanksgiving, I asked Molly if she would like me to transfer the soup we had for lunch from the stove to the back porch to cool. She replied, "I'll probably fix you a steak for supper, and I may eat the soup." I was left to interpret what that means. Did it answer my question? Perhaps in a manner of speaking, but very obliquely. A simple "yes" or "no" would do quite nicely, thank you. This happens a lot to which I often reply, "But that doesn't answer the question I asked." Then she will answer the question directly. Does this happen to anybody else? It isn't necessarily wrong. It's just a difference to be considered and navigated.

Men tend to be blunt, brief, and to the point. With a smaller daily allocation of words ourselves, we are perhaps not as inclined to listen at length either. However, sometimes a deal is struck. As someone suggested, men have been known to strive to be better listeners in hopes that it will lead to sex. In reverse, women sometimes will allow sex hoping it will lead to conversation!

Who's In Control?

Everybody knows the effects of heredity and environment that combine to give us our makeup. Author and motivational speaker, Brian Tracy, said, "Women are complex and subtle. Men are simple and direct." Business leader, Jeff Yager seemed to concur by saying, "Men are wired to work and be a warrior. Men are simple minded and beam their focus. Women, instead, are wired for family." Jeff added that women are multi-taskers. They can handle many pots on the stove and children noisily running around underfoot. With the onset of wifehood and motherhood, women tend to become more task-oriented and take-charge. It is their nature to do so in response to their new, varied, and essential roles. Many a full blooded, macho man has claimed to have the last word. Ha! Often, it's, "Yes Dear!"

Trying to cheer her husband up after a rough day at work, a wife proclaimed, "Honey, look at it this way. You may be low man on the totem pole at work, but here at home, you're number two in command!" Keep in mind ladies, men do not like to be micromanaged or directed about too many minor details. In fact, Birdie Yager, wife of my mentor Dexter, has cautioned, "The strong-willed woman, who insists everything be done her way, may be destroying her marriage, her man, and her future."

Women taking charge is a result of the responsibilities of marriage and motherhood. Another friend and business associate, Ed Courtney said, in essence, "Men want sex while women want control." Women have their subtle ways to get what they want. For example, one wife said to her husband, "OK, if you don't want to take me to the movies, we'll stay home. I have some wonderful ideas for rearranging the living room furniture."

A few years ago, *Readers Digest* published the results of a worldwide study asking, "Who is in charge of the home?" In the United States, where the majority of women work outside the home, 60% of responders said, "Mom calls the shots!" In Germany, the answer was "Grandparents." China, Singapore, and the United Kingdom said, "Kids rule the roost!"

I have often joked (perhaps representing the position of many men) that I make the BIG decisions at our house — like how to handle immigration, what to do about the troubles in the Middle East, and concerns about our national debt — the really important stuff. Molly handles most of the day-to-day operations, the more mundane things about running our household — major purchases, scheduling, and planning, basically where we go and what we do. How would I ever manage without Molly doing so many things? Answer: not very well. I am constantly amazed at her work ethic and productivity level, and how much she accomplishes, about most of which, I don't seem to have a clue.

Men on the other hand, often become more passive, less assertive, more mellow, and more agreeable with age, even though they may be set in their ways. They get worn down by striving, work demands, disagreements, stress, financial responsibilities and competition. We eventually come to overlook more. We decide to "just let it go" in the interest of peace.

In midlife, a man went to a marriage counselor who asked, "What first attracted you to your wife?"

The man replied, "I liked her decisiveness."

The counselor then asked, "Why then, are you now tell-ing me you want to end your relationship?"

The man replied, "Because of her decisiveness."

Further illustrating this trait of control, I heard a story of a dying man on his death bed. He was discussing with his wife his final wishes and the roles of their children. He said, "I'd like to put George in charge of the store."

The wife replied, "You know, Walt is better suited. He's smarter."

Next the man said, "I want to give Jim the van."

His wife then added, "Really, Tom needs it more, with his big family."

The man continued by suggesting, "Let Shirley have the lake house."

To which the wife pointed out, "You know how Shirley hates the water. Give it to Beth."

Finally in desperation the man groaned, "Who's dying, you or me?"

Birdie Yager once again warned, "When a woman denies

her man the freedom to make choices, to act on his dreams, she is denying him his very masculinity."

Preferences

(1) THINGS—Someone calculated that a man has 6 things in his bathroom: a toothbrush and toothpaste, shaving cream, a razor, a comb, and a bar of soap. On the other hand, the average number of items in a typical woman's bathroom is 297. Furthermore, a man probably would not even be able to identify more than 15 of those.

(2) PARTIES—As Ann Landers said, "At every party there are two kinds of people: those who want to go home and those who don't. The trouble is, they are usually married to each other." This is yet another confirmation that opposites attract. Some have said, while it may be true that opposites attract, they then attack.

(3) FOOTBALL—A husband fell asleep in front of the TV watching Monday Night Football. The next morning his wife pokes him, in alarm at the time, and exclaims, "It's 20 to 7!"

He asks excitedly, "In whose favor?"

Irritated, the wife replies, "I sometimes think you love football more than you love me."

"Yes, dear, but I do love you more than basketball."

There's more. The Super Bowl was over, finally ending the football season. The fanatical fan reluctantly turned off the TV with a sigh, looked around the den, and

discovered that his wife had left him in November!

A friend I was watching games with on New Year's Day told a timely story about a young bride's first introduction to that day devoted to college football. He laughingly told that her husband had spent all day sitting in front of the TV, watching the games. The only time he said anything to her was when he asked for more beer and pretzels. Finally, the bride could no longer bear being ignored. In a huff (which he barely noticed as he was unwilling to shift his eyes from the game), she said, "I'm going over to Mother's. Maybe she'll talk to me." Much to her surprise, however, when she arrived, she found her father there alone, engrossed in the same game her husband had been watching. Her mother was over at HER mother's house. Ha!

Finally, to add insult to injury, one more story to make a point. A guy gets a ticket to the Super Bowl but finds his seat is way up in the nosebleed section. He looks around for a better seat. He spots an empty seat down on the fifty-yard line and runs down to possibly claim it. "What a view!" he exclaims to the elderly man seated next to him. "Why would anyone pass this up?"

"It's my wife's seat" says the older man. "We've gone to every Super Bowl since we were married, but she passed away."

"I'm so sorry," says the new occupant, "Couldn't you find a friend to come with you?"

The elder man shakes his head and says, "No, they are all at her funeral."

Two hilarious examples of differences, which came to me in emails and which by the suggestive tone of them, were probably written by men.

TEN reasons why men prefer GUNS over WOMEN.

1. You can trade an old 44 for a new 22.

2. You can keep one gun at home and have another for when you are on the road.

3. If you admire a friend's gun and tell him so, he will probably let you try it out a few times.

4. Your primary gun doesn't mind if you keep another gun for back up.

5. Your gun will stay with you even if you run out of ammunition.

6. A gun doesn't take up a lot of space in a closet.

7. Guns function normally every day of the month.

8. A gun doesn't ask "Do these new grips make me look fat?"

9. A gun doesn't mind if you go to sleep after you use it.

10. You can buy a silencer for your gun!

Along a similar vein is this e-mail I received: *Why Men Like Airplanes*

- Airplanes kill you quickly; a woman may take years.

- Airplanes can be turned on at the flick of a switch.

- Airplanes don't get mad if you do a touch and go.

- Airplanes don't object to a preflight inspection.

- Airplanes come with a manual to explain how they operate.

- Airplanes have strict weight and balance limitations.

- Airplanes don't come with in-laws.

- Airplanes don't care how many other planes you've flown before.
- Airplanes and pilots both arrive at the same time.
- Airplanes don't mind if you look at other airplanes.
- Airplanes don't mind if you buy airplane magazines.
- Airplanes expect to be tied down.
- Airplanes don't comment on your piloting skills.
- Airplanes don't whine unless something is really wrong.
- However, when airplanes go quiet, just like women, it's a bad sign.

Expectations of a Marriage

My college roommate Al used to always say, "Anticipation is greater than realization." Perhaps that is true of many things. In marriage, it depends on the couple. It is true that with marriage, there comes more responsibility, and you can count on many more surprises as well. Men marry women expecting that this sweet young thing they love will remain the same sweet submissive person. She doesn't. Women marry men with numerous ideas, under the guise of being helpful. How can she work on this guy to change and improve him?

Men need to continue to be the leader of the household and not just give in and become a wimp. Remember, women like a man who takes control, otherwise they will! He may silently submit, in the interest of keeping the peace, but he may internally build up resentment over time about being dominated. We have known two couples who ostensibly seemed to get along. Then suddenly in midlife, to the wife's total surprise, the husband up and left. It happens just like in that popular Glen Campbell happy-sad song "By the Time I Get to Phoenix." Such break ups should not come as a surprise, since the handwriting is on the wall for all but the most imperceptive to see.

Crucial Communication Styles

In any good relationship, it is necessary to have open communication, growth together, and cooperative give and take. In one of his daily devotionals, pastor David Jeremiah said that understanding leads to love and likewise love leads to understanding. The crucial ingredient in such a merging of minds is open, honest, and rational communication. Alfred Adler expressed it this way, "He who feels loved, feels understood and he who feels understood, feels loved."

I have always thought that two people could say anything to each other so long as it was said with good intent, and verbalized calmly without anger, high pitched volume, run away emotion, or hysteria. We choose how to accept messages we receive from others. We can choose to be offended or take what may be said to us, even if critical or in a derogatory way, with a certain degree of humble introspection instead.

Of course, that is not easy. It means biting one's tongue and counting to ten before responding softly. In a state of defensiveness, you may want to lash back, but silence or a calm response often leads to a more positive resolution. When either party decides to be offended and storm out of a room, slam down the phone, or just turn their back and walk off, that ends further dialogue and, with it, any hope of resolving the conflict. It's certainly easier and more natural to respond in kind. However, one must ask: which is more likely to produce a positive result — storming out or continuing to communicate? The Good Book says that when struck, turn the other cheek. Hard enough to do but worth doing. Impossible to do though, if one chooses to be offended!

Becoming One from Two

"Keep your eyes wide open before marriage, half shut afterwards," said wise old Ben Franklin in his popular Poor Richards' Almanac. A perfect wife is one who doesn't expect a perfect husband and vice versa. English author W. Somerset Maugham said,

> *American women expect to find in their husbands*
> *a perfection that English women only hope to find*
> *in their butlers.*

Seems to me that a worthy goal in marriage should be for BOTH parties to be happy, not just one of you. This means several things. "What counts in making a happy marriage is not so much how compatible you are, but how you deal with incompatibility," said psychology professor George Levinger. "The meeting of two personalities is like the contact of two chemical substances: if there is any reaction, both are transformed," said psychologist Carl Jung. Therefore, be this known to all, "you don't just marry one person," said Canadian humorist, Richard Needham. "You marry three: the person you think they are, the person they are, and the person they are going to become as a result of being married to you." Wow! That's influence to think about, isn't it?

Desires of the Heart

I had a conversation with a friend about what three things every woman wants. FIRST and foremost, women want a friend. With Molly and I, our friendship preceded our marriage. With a successful marriage, friendship develops and intensifies with time as husband and wife successfully meet the challenges of life together. A lasting marital relationship could depend more on liking than on loving, as familiarity naturally develops. The passionate love that one has in their youth is incomplete and superficial compared to that of an old man for his wife and an old woman for her husband.

Here's a beautiful analogy of walking on the rail of the railroad track and the power of a friend. We have all done this as kids and learned you can't walk very far teetering on the rail if you look at your feet. Walking on the rail, just as in a in a marriage, one does better when you get your head up and look far down the track long term, to where you are going (toward your dreams and goals). Then for maximum distance upon balancing the rails, you get on one rail and your life partner and best friend on the other. As you reach across to each other for support, holding hands, you can overcome balance problems and walk on the rails (and in life) as far as you want. Wherefore, 1+1=2, 1 and 1 side by side equals 11. Working together enhances the odds for success.

Be a team of two. Several times in our life, when Molly and I faced disappointment and discouragement, we have sung that old song whose words are "It's you and me against the world..." Life in general, and married life in particular, is a long series of overcoming best faced together. As Kate Stewart said, "The perfect marriage is just two imperfect people who refuse to give up on each other." In other words, according to Ruth Bell Graham, "A happy marriage is the union of two good forgivers." Samuel Coleridge humorously said, "The most happy marriage I can picture or imagine to myself would be the union of a deaf man to a blind woman."

The SECOND thing a woman wants is a lover. The ancient Greeks came up with seven words to delineate different kinds of love. You may be familiar with them.

EROS—romantic, passionate love

PHILIA—intimate, authentic friendship love

LUDUS—playful, flirtatious love

STORGE—unconditional, familial love

PHILAUTIA—self love

PRAGMA—committed, passionate love

AGAPE—empathetic, universal love

How many of these apply to husband and wife? Would you say perhaps all but Philautia (self-love) and Agape (universal love)? Certainly, true love is long lasting rather than temporary, deep rooted rather than superficial, focused on one rather than many, and the interests of your mate rather than yourself. Love is more than a feeling; love is a commitment and a decision that does not change. We are to love, honor, and nourish our mates as we would love our own body. "Husbands, love your wives, even as Christ also loved the church, and gave himself for it" (Ephesians 5:25).

The person you love may not be perfect, but they may

be perfect for you. Keep in mind that your mate may not be perfect but then, admit it, neither are you. A popular song a few years back was entitled "Love and Marriage." In it was the line, "Love and marriage, you can't have one without the other." Well, I guess you can, but then what?

True love in marriage must be based on more than just feelings, since feelings can be both superficial and fleeting. As mentioned earlier, like happiness and success, love is a decision. A person chooses to love another and must keep making that choice even if they don't "feel it" at the moment.

To love someone requires a decision. As Sam Keen once said, "We come to love not by finding a perfect person but by learning to see an imperfect person perfectly." I suppose the expression "falling in love" originated because it often happens by accident and causes one to seem helpless, out of control like physically falling, captivated by romantic circumstances. You may have asked: what about that tingly feeling you get when you are falling in love? That is common sense leaving your body.

The reality is that women fall in love with their ears. A man, however, falls in love with his eyes. Attending a bridal shower for a friend that was getting married, my wife Molly asked the bride to be why she had chosen this man instead of any of the others she had dated. She answered that she had been impressed with several who appeared bright, personable, and special. When she was with her intended however, HE made HER feel bright, personable, and special.

A lover doesn't brood over the past. A lover is content with the present and hopes for the future. Lovers have an interdependent confidence. Lovers mutually forgive. Lovers share both good and bad times. Lovers have common goals. Lovers are loyal to each other.

THIRD among a woman's desires is a protector. Women are security-oriented. They want to be cared for and nurtured. They want to be protected from their fears. They want a protector who will handle things. They want a protector who will treat disasters like incidents and no incident like a disaster. They want a protector who will be calm under pressure. They want a protector who will hold the umbrella over them in the rain. They want a protector who opens the car door for them and closes it after them. They want a protector who will step into the boat first then hold out his hand and help her in. All common courtesies perhaps, but important to her. Chivalrous too.

Most young girls dream that, like Snow White, someday her handsome prince will come, her knight in shining armor to take care of her and protect her. That's where we men come in.

Getting Along

Some might say overlooking minor irritations is simply "choosing your battles." I've also heard it said that marriage is nature's way of preventing you from fighting with total strangers! Common marital advice cautions, "Don't go to bed angry." Phyllis Diller agreed but then added, "Stay up and fight it out." A clue here, guys, is to let a woman have the last word in an argument. Anything a man says after that either escalates the volume or starts the next argument.

According to my friend Jerry Meadows, it pays BIG

dividends in your relationship with your wife if you learn to say three things: Yes Dear, I'll listen, and I'm sorry. Then he should repeat two sentences as often as possible: "I love you" and "I need you." Jerry also said, "It works wonders to say every now and then, 'Let's you and I just go sit and talk a little while.'" Birdie Yager added that, "Words are awfully important to a woman. Men, tell her how you feel about her, how much you appreciate her, and love her." Lift each other up. Compliment one another.

On a humorous note, men, please remember that marital research clearly shows that heavy, overweight women do live longer than their husbands who keep pointing that out to their wives! A wife said to her husband, "I have a bag full of used clothing I'd like to donate."

The husband answered, "Why not just throw it in the trash? That is much easier."

The wife pleaded her case by saying, "But there are poor starving people who can really use all these clothes."

The husband replied, "Honey, anyone who can fit into your clothes is not starving."

The husband is now recovering from a head injury. That guy is in the hospital room right across the hall from the husband who said to his out-of-town wife on the phone, "I'm so miserable without you, it's almost as if you are here."

Perhaps on whichever side of the aisle we find ourselves, we need to remember marriage is not static. It is a work in progress. Author and speaker Ron Ball, in one of his marriage seminars said, "Marriage is not a noun; it's a verb. It isn't something you get. It is something you do. It's the way you love your partner every day." To emphasize that point, someone suggested that marriage is a two-way street that is always under construction. I've learned that in Minneapolis they say there are just two seasons. One is the long, cold winter. The other season is known as "construction." Robert Rohm said in one of his Tip of the Week emails, "Life is simply a series of mid-course crashes. Sorry, I meant to say corrections."

Since the home is the dwelling place of a marriage, it needs to be a safe harbor in times of storms. It should be a place of tranquility rather than a producer of anxiety. A friend of mine was relating a discussion he was having with his wife about the sharing of duties at home. My friend said he thought household responsibilities were pretty equally divided. His wife however, felt unequally overworked. He said they debated a while when she said, "I do things around the house that you don't even know about."

He then said, "Yeah, like what?"

She immediately clinched it with, "See, I told you."

A story from Bits and Pieces tells of a woman seeking counsel from Dr. George W. Crane, the psychologist. She confided that she hated her husband and intended to divorce him. "I want to hurt him all I can," she declared firmly.

"Well in that case," said Dr. Crane, "I advise you to start showering him with compliments. When you have become indispensable to him, when he thinks you love him devotedly, then start divorce action. That is the way to hurt him."

Some months later the wife returned to report that all was going well. She had followed his instructions to the letter. "Good," said Dr. Crane. "Now is the time to execute your plan and surprise him with divorce papers."

"Oh no!" said the wife. "I couldn't do that now. We are getting along so great. We are like newlyweds again." Dr. Crane smiled.

A few years ago, *Readers Digest* published a survey asking married couples if they would marry the same person again. Saying "yes" were those in China at 83%, Germany 73%, United Kingdom 66%, United States 63% and the lowest was Malaysia at 59%. Getting along is a decision. You simply decide to get along, just like you choose to be happy, and like you choose to love someone.

Typical of the many heartfelt quotes and stories coming from Bits and Pieces is this one, on the topic of getting along. I don't think that many women, when angered, could remain as silent as long and for as many times as the woman in this story. Weeks before his wife's 75th birthday, a man decided to buy his wife a new hat to wear to church on Sundays. Unfortunately, he didn't know her hat size and decided to check one that was in her closet. He retrieved an old worn hat box from the top shelf of the closet and almost fainted when he opened it. Inside the box were two lace doilies and wads of cash. He sat down and counted out the bills, all $85,653 of them.

When his wife returned home that afternoon, she found her husband sitting at the dining room table with the money in neat little stacks and a confused expression on his face. "What is the meaning of this?" he asked.

"Every time I was angry with you, I made a doily," she said, as she patted his hand and walked into the kitchen to start dinner.

The husband looked to his wife of over 50 years, and his

eyes began to moisten. He held the two doilies in his hand and smiled at her. And then, he asked, "Where did all that money come from?"

She answered, "It's what I made from selling the doilies."

The Seasons of Marriage

When we are first married (the honeymoon years, as they are known), everything is usually blissful. During that time, passions of new love are blossoming because our DESIRE for each other is being fulfilled. Then as the years go by, we settle into the focus on child rearing, career progression, paying the bills, making ends meet, and just generally having to cope with life's circumstances and problems.

Therefore, the middle years become the most CRITI-CAL. They are most critical because, with the accompanying pressures, they could easily become the most volatile. Then too, they could perhaps become the other extreme. That is, a marriage over time could evolve into a routine, dull, boring, and unexciting lifestyle, which is perhaps even more stifling. This is also the danger zone of the 40's and the "seven-year itch."

After weathering all the storms of mid-life, comes the latter years when, more than any other time in marriage, two people really NEED each other, as health declines and old age sets in. Old age becomes prime time to get along and be kind to one another. Because of the physical challenges it brings, there is a book by Art Linkletter which aptly describes the latter years called, Old Age Is Not for Sissies.

In the summer of 1968, I had a graduate fellowship at

Arizona State University. During that summer we travelled extensively throughout the southwest. I came across a plaque with these beautiful words below. It seems so well to cover this subject of getting along in marriage, I would like to include it as inspiration. The words seem to represent the thoughts and sentiments of "the noble savage" rather than the image we were taught in history of the fierce, tough, sometimes cruel Apache warrior. Here is the tender and sentimental Apache Wedding Blessing.

Now you will feel no rain, for each of you will be shelter for the other.

Now you will feel no cold, for each of you will be warmth for the other.

Now there is no more loneliness, for each of you will be a companion to the other.

Now you are two persons but there is only one life before you.

May your days together be good and long upon the earth.

Enduring Love

Will Durant said,

> The love we have in our youth is superficial compared to the love that an old man has for his old wife.

And I might add, the love an old wife has for her husband. In human relations, being as tenuous as it can be with some people, love in our youth or love at first sight is understandable. It is in old age after two people have been together as marrieds for decades, that such a relationship becomes a miracle. Well, not really. Because of a firm and lasting commitment to each other, old marrieds have conquered so many obstacles, have had (several to numerous) high volume discussions, managed to find agreement after disagreements, fought off enemies together, and stood united against the world as overcomers. They are bonded together like comrades in arms.

Author Robert Rohm maintains there is no such thing as unconditional love. He says we should learn to love people sacrificially. If you love people sacrificially, you will keep on loving them! You will learn to forgive, and you will realize we all cause heartache and pain to others at different times, and you will keep on loving them anyway. Sacrificial love is the best love of all.

Life is made of memories. Marriage is made of shared memories meant to be remembered, reviewed, and savored. That thought brings back music to my ears from the classic MGM movie, Gigi. The entertaining, beautiful, and inspiring music was written by Lerner and Loewe. Although they had trouble coming up with matching memories, who could forget Maurice Chevalier and Hermione Gingold when they sang to each other that humorous but sentimental old song, "I Remember It Well." Such memories for any two people so long in love are truly a blessing.

My beautiful, smart, well organized, competent, and sweet daughter Virginia met the love of her life Ed in her fifties. Ed is handsome, personable, extremely smart, and very well-suited for Virginia. I know she would say that she wished she had met him sooner so she could have loved him longer, as she is happier than I have ever seen her in her adult years. I would say the same thing about Molly, my bride of

63 years at this writing. In a happy marriage, your mate is your best friend—someone you pray for, someone you are thankful for every night, and someone you need and depend upon. I don't know how I would make it through the day, let alone a month or a year, without her. She has become the most valuable person in the world to me! As my friend Steve Yager said about his beautiful wife Cici, "There is magic in being needed by the person you love most."

Dexter cautioned men in his book titled, *Pursuit*, "If you don't learn to love your wife, then you may never give your daughters a reason to love you." Father Theodore Hesburgh, former President of Notre Dame University so wisely cast a father's role this way, "The most important thing a father can do for his children is to love their mother." Birdie Yager added, "It is difficult for parents to show love for their children if they don't show love to each other."

I'd like to end this segment with two stories, one funny and one inspiring. The first is about an enduring love, but not necessarily for the same person.

I was told about an eighty-year-old lady in a small town who was getting married. The local paper thought this was newsworthy and sent out a reporter to interview her. "Tell me about your husband to be," said the reporter.

"We'll, he's a funeral director."

"That's interesting. Have you ever been married before?" the reporter asked.

"Yes," she replied. "Actually, three times."

The reporter suddenly became even more interested. "Can you tell me about that?"

"Of course. At age 20, I fell in love with a wealthy banker, but he was sedentary, got fat, and died early of a heart attack. I took a few years to get over that so that by age 40, I met and married a circus performer. He was a tightrope artist. One day there was an accident. He fell and was killed. Twenty years later I met and married my third husband. He was a preacher. Wonderful man but he also passed all too soon."

The reporter was amazed and commented, "How diverse and unusual. Now at age 80 you are marrying your fourth husband, the undertaker. How do you explain all that – a banker, a circus performer, a preacher and finally an undertaker?"

The old lady smiled and said, "One for the money, two for the show, three to get ready, and four to go!"

Now, another story from Bits and Pieces of enduring love in medieval Bavaria, where a castle filled with riches came under attack. The invading army was strong and claimed victory over the castle, its inhabitants, and its treasures. The men of the castle reluctantly accepted their defeat and were prepared to surrender. But their wives had other plans. With their lives and wealth at stake, the women decided to negotiate their own truce with the invaders. Ultimately, it was agreed that the women would be guaranteed safe passage from the castle with whatever possessions they could carry out themselves.

The castle gates opened, and the women walked out slowly. Their backs were bent under the weight of their most valued possessions. At the sight of these brave wives, the soldiers of the conquering army were moved to tears. The invaders knew that the women wouldn't be able to remove all of the treasures the castle held. Yet, it never occurred to them what the women considered to be their true wealth. Each wife had left behind all her gold, jewels, and other material possessions. They were bent over struggling to carry out the weight of their husbands on their backs.

Now that is an example of true love, lasting love, enduring love.

Our Ultimate Relationship

Molly and I met in New Hampshire in 1958, where I was the Waterfront Director at a very successful summer boys camp on Lake Winnipesaukee. One summer, Molly came up from South Carolina as the waterskiing counselor at the sister girls camp nearby.

From the early counselor "get acquainted" dance, soon after the opening of camp in June, we dated every other night. The hit movie that summer was High Society staring Bing Crosby and Grace Kelly. It featured that beautiful Cole Porter song, entitled "True Love," which we adopted as our song. We knew "this was it" for both of us. That summer was my fourth summer at the camp, so I knew the owners really well. They were very cautious when I shared with them that I had met the girl I wanted to marry. I was 28 and Molly was 19. They said, "You better slow down and be careful. She is from the south and you are from the north." Then they added kiddingly, "You don't even speak the same language." (The southern accent was much more prevalent in speech back then, but American English has been greatly homogenized by TV since.)

The owners meant well in giving me their advice. Actually, in many such North-South relationships they might have been correct. However, what they didn't know was that, even though we grew up 650 miles apart and on opposite sides of the "Mason-Dixon line," we were raised with similar values. We looked at things the same way. We came from families that raised us to be Christians and political conservatives. (By the way, when dating and seeking a mate, sometime during the courting process, don't hesitate to discuss the fundamental issues of politics and religion. They form a powerful foundation for either ultimate togetherness or eventual divisiveness.)

We were on the same page. All we had to work out between us were any personality idiosyncrasies and the normal issues of dealing with life's day to day circumstances. Our upbringing helped us to "click" in terms of communication and understanding between us. With no exceptions, getting married will solve some problems, but it will create infinitely more. Only through the framework of open, honest communications, in pursuit of common goals, can those ongoing problems be solved.

Dixieland Culture

At the end of the summer of '58 when Pat Boone sang his hit songs of "Love Letters in the Sand" and "Old Cape Cod," Molly went back to South Carolina where she was a student at the University of South Carolina. I went back to suburban Philadelphia where I was an Assistant Principal at a high school there. That fall, having come from a historically prominent family in South Carolina, Molly was in the process of making her debut in society. There were three formal Debutante Balls from October through December. I was able to escort her to two of them. Molly was not allowed to become officially engaged until all three dances had been completed. She secretly carried the engagement ring I gave her in her purse. Our love and friendship continued to grow via letters, occasional visits back and forth, and long-distance phone calls. We saved those letters for over 60 years, hoping to read them again late in life. It is now late in our life, but unfortunately, the box of all those romantic letters was lost in our recent move.

During my first trip to "Dixieland" in the fall of 1958, I was introduced to Molly's family. Her father was a southern gentleman and an attorney. He told me a lawyer joke that old lawyers never die, they just lose their appeal. Since I was an educator, I countered with, old principals never die, they just lose their faculties. He liked that. Her family went back to the founding fathers of our country, the Continental Congress, the writing of our nation's founding documents and the Revolutionary War. Her family had a long tradition of southern culture.

For example, in my early discussions with Molly's father, he let it be known to me that he didn't know until he was 25 years old that "Damn Yankee" was two words. After that, I was careful what I said and decided it would be best if I were to put on my return address, the name Roland Lee Hughes, (the Lee being for that revered southern hero and gentleman General Robert E.)

When the final Ball was over, I met with Molly's father to formally ask his approval for us to marry. He was very nice about accepting a Yankee into the family, which was my clue to level with him. I said, "I suppose you have noticed that on my return address I listed my name as Roland Lee Hughes."

He smiled and nodded affirmatively being reminded of the dear departed General. Then I said, "I need to tell you that my middle name is not Lee. My middle name is Grant." It was like he was dumbstruck. His lips moved, but no words came out. Finally, after a good 30 seconds, he finally said, "Well, at least that's better than Sherman," who you may remember from your American History in eleventh grade. He is the infamous Yankee General who burned Atlanta, then lead a scorched earth band of destruction to Columbia, South Carolina, and whose cannon shells have left pock marks in the capital building. To this day the name Sherman is "mud" to any true southerner.

Another interesting historical side note about Sherman connects with the First Baptist Church in Columbia where we have been members since 1972. The original building of which is where the Articles of Secession were signed to begin the Civil War. Sherman rode up to the church intent on burning it. The black custodian of the church stepped out to meet the mounted troopers with torches. Sherman asked if this was the First Baptist Church where the articles were signed. The custodian said, "No Sir," and directed Sherman and his troops around the corner to the Methodist Church, which they gladly burned to the ground.

So, that is how we began. We had some differences, of course — nothing major, all were manageable. Mostly, we had commonalities. Dexter taught that a person gets better by concentrating on their strengths. Sure, you work on your weaknesses and faults to improve, but that should not be one's major focus. Success in anything, as an individual, comes from building on your strengths, finding and using your God-given talents and putting them to work serving other people. The same is true in developing a marital relationship. We became friends then progressed to become best friends for life. So often, as God puts a couple together, He blends the strengths of one to balance the weaknesses of the other and vice versa. Such complementing one another is the positive part of, and great strength of, opposites attracting.

Choice for Life

In college I had a friend that lived across the hall. Bob was very handsome, athletic, and well liked. He looked like a Marine Corps recruiting poster. Our college had a Marine Corps summer training program. Candidates trained at Quantico, Virginia, in the summers after both their sophomore and junior years. Then, upon graduation from college, they would be commissioned as a second lieutenant followed by several years of enlistment. Bob went through that program. He made a career of the Marines, was wounded in the Korean war, lost an arm, but rose to the rank of Major General.

Here is the point of this story. Through all four years of college, he dated a pretty girl named Barbara. He told me he was going to marry her right after graduation during the interim before going into the "Old Corps." I congratulated him and wished him happiness. Here's the shocker. Do you know what he said to me next? He kind of looked at his shoes and said something to the effect that, "Well after going with her for four years, it would be too difficult to break up now. It is just easier to marry her." I was flabbergasted. I thought what a terrible thought process to have entering into marriage. From what I heard, I guess they stayed married, but how happily I don't know. I think they lived apart much of their marriage as his duties in the military probably took priority over the marriage relationship. In essence, I suppose, Bob was married to "The Corps."

Then while I was a professor of education at the University of South Carolina, I encountered a similar approach to marriage. One of the couples who met in my class, and that I got to know well, informed me they were going to get married upon graduation. I had the opportunity to talk to him privately about that upcoming event in their life. He shocked me by saying, "Yeah, we're going to get married, and I hope things work out. But if they don't, I can find somebody else." Wow! Again, what a lousy sense of commitment in which to enter matrimony. If I remember correctly, the vows say, "for better or worse, until death do us part."

My college roommate was a popular, good looking, athletic, and gregarious fellow. He dated many nice girls during his college years and probably could have married any one of them. As noted, opposites attract. Who Al chose to marry, instead of one of our classmates, was a girl from his old city neighborhood.

Geri was pretty, a meticulous housekeeper, a great organizer, and a most industrious worker. She wanted everything to be perfect. Her modus operandi was neatness with a capital N! Add to that, she had trouble being happy. Al, in turn, was an optimistic, happy-go-lucky guy and less concerned about neatness and order. Although, he was certainly neat enough to be a Marine officer. During his mid-fifties he confessed to me that there were constant tensions between them, and they really didn't get along. He said though, that he didn't believe in divorce and had resigned himself to the fact that he was going to "live out his life in quiet desperation." It saddened me. He died shortly thereafter of a heart attack.

It is easy to think, in the heat of the romancing process, of how great it would be to be married. It is essential to force oneself to think long term. After all, coming together is a beginning, staying together makes for progress, finishing united is true success. As Ron Ball said, "The Golden Rule of marriage, and the secret of making love last through the years, is simply being kind to one another."

The Ultimate Disaster

So, we go from our ultimate relationship of love at first sight, a happy marriage of 63 years, and a choice for life, to consider the other extreme — of conflict, unhappiness, hurt, unkindness, vengeance, separation, regrets, and divorce. Thus we get the expression, "Divorce never, murder maybe." As mentioned earlier, the divorce or separation rate is close to 50%. This then becomes a viable, easier to obtain, and an increasingly acceptable alternative to continuing in an unhappy marriage. The public stigma formerly attached to divorce seems to have abated since World War II, as evidenced by the proliferation of divorces. Multiple marriages are more commonplace, no longer confined to those of convenience by the Hollywood crowd.

I don't remember who first told me these jokes, but I have been telling them for years and have taken possession of them, as though they were my own. Along with aging myself, I have taken an increasing interest in geriatric humor. So, there was a 95-year-old man who went to see a divorce attorney. The surprised attorney asked, "Why do you want a divorce now at your stage of life, having been married for 75 years?"

The old man replied, "Well, if the truth be known, our marriage has been on the rocks for years, but we didn't want to get a divorce until all the children died."

On the subject of old age, I have usually told two stories in tandem. The second of the two has little to do with the subject bearing of this chapter. However, since I have always told these two stories as a pair, I will do so here, and throw in the companion joke free of charge. It seems that a 95-year-old man went to see a sex therapist. He complained to the therapist that he wasn't getting the same joy and zinger out of sex. It just wasn't as good anymore. The therapist noted his age and asked, "When did he first notice this diminishing response?"

The old man replied, "Well, last night and again this morning!"

When I told that story to my friend Wendell, he said, "We should all be so fortunate." I think so too, don't you?

Returning to the subject at hand — of the ultimate disasters in marriage — brings up the main theme of this book, namely that of making choices. So many aspects of life begin with a decision, consciously contrived or imposed unconsciously by circumstance. Faced with diminishing love, increased conflicts, greater stress, and continuing unhappiness, what to do? In examining the choices, there are few.

a-Accept the situation in which you find yourself and

tough it out. (Like my roommate Al who chose to live out his life in "quiet desperation.")

b-Take the initiative to resolve issues, getting professional help from someone whose goal is to help you stay together rather than a counselor whose philosophy is freedom of self. Some counselors, those who are not biblically-based philosophically, lean toward enabling the easy way out.

c-Choose divorce. With that choice be reminded that, in most cases where children are involved, divorce is never final. It also is damaging to the children who often find themselves in a war zone, torn between two parents. Unless one party abdicates all parental responsibility and migrates to a foreign country to have a new life, in the future, both parties will still have to interact with one another. This is not only in the immediate divorce proceedings and settlement arrangements, but also in every future celebration event in the lives of their children, which brings the divorcees together again and again. Additionally, monetary issues are seldom equitable for both parties. "Deadbeat Dads" are a dime a dozen.

The biggest losers in divorces always are the children. Dennis Delisle writes in *Calling the Called*, while "only 30% of all US kids come from broken homes, it turns out that these unfortunate victims of divorce account for over 70% of our prison population, 60% of rapists, 75% of adolescents charged with murder, and 80% of those classified as motivated by displaced anger."

Molly and I recently met an attractive, young, divorced woman with two young children. She came from Korea and, once here, married a young American Korean man. She found out after the birth of their two children that he was irresponsible, and she divorced him. He provided nothing for her nor for the children. She was entirely on her own having no family in this country. She had no choice but to tough it out, and she has. She is one smart and enterprising young lady.

This is getting heavy, as it needs to be, since this is sobering, serious stuff. That means it is time for a story or two to lighten up the narrative. It seems that a highway patrolman pulled over a speeder but not until a chase of several miles had occurred. Finally apprehended, the driver said to the officer, "Please, sir, don't give me a ticket."

The officer countered with, "You deserve two. One for the original speed you were going and two, for the chase. I'll give you a warning if you have a good excuse."

The driver said, "My wife ran off with a highway patrolman last year, and I thought you were bringing her back." The patrolman laughed and no ticket was issued.

Then there was the story of a patient whose doctor told him he had only six months to live. The patient was shocked at such a short time. He asked if there was anything he could do to stretch out the time?

The doctor couldn't think of anything to do medically. Then he got an idea. He said, "Perhaps I could arrange for you to live with my ex-wife in Florida for six months. Living with her for six months would seem like an eternity."

In 1973, Ed Young was the pastor of the First Baptist Church, in Columbia, South Carolina, where we attended. This was before he left to become the pastor of the Second Baptist Church in Houston, Texas and nationally renowned as a gifted preacher on TV. Before he left, one of his sermons dealt with marriage and divorce. I clearly remember him giving his opinion as to the two major causes of divorce.

The first cause, he said, was an attitude of selfishness rather than selflessness. Remember, the aim of marriage is to make each other happy. Dexter always said to treat your wife like a queen and she will treat you like a king. Each is to care for, be kind to, and uplift the other.

Secondly, Pastor Young said that the other major contributor to divorce was finances. The financial battleground results, of course, from insufficient funds or -more accurately - living above your means. It doesn't matter so much how much income there is in a family, but whether one chooses to live within or below their means. Being broke is not so much about an amount but rather about attitude and choices. More about finances later under other choices.

Molly and I know a smart, industrious, frugal, and disciplined young couple, David and Sunnae, who successfully raised and educated five children on an assistant pastors' salary. To succeed in such a situation requires clear goals, self-discipline, self-sacrifice, and an understanding of delayed gratification.

A reverse example of financial choices occurred in a family with which we are very familiar. The man had a very successful career in the medical field and was retired. Two of his children have never learned financial discipline. They constantly lived above their means, they never had saved funds to meet emergencies, and they consistently made bad personal and financial decisions. This continued for years because they had been taught by their father that they could come pleading to him for money, and he would give it to them. His innate nature of generosity worked against him in the long run, teaching his children to be poor financial managers, irresponsible, and overly dependent on him well into adulthood. One of these grown children in this situation is divorced, while the other is still married, but one might say unsatisfactorily so. Both grown children have lived in a world of anxiety, conflict, and unhappiness. As Jim Rohn said, "We must all suffer from one of two pains: the pain of discipline or the pain of regret. The difference is discipline weighs ounces while regret weighs tons."

Joyce Brothers once quipped, "My husband and I have never considered divorce… murder sometimes, but never divorce." I'll use two stories to illustrate that remark and to make a humorous point. It was a well-known fact in England during Churchill's time that he and the socially elite Lady Astor did not like each other. Once Lady Astor told Churchill that if she were his wife, she would poison his tea. Churchill, with his quick wit, had a clever reply. He said, "Madam, if I was your husband, I'd gladly drink it!"

Ellen Sanders tells a story of six guys who are playing poker. When Smith loses $500 on a single hand, he clutches his chest and falls over dead. Who is going to tell his wife, they all wonder? So, they draw straws and Anderson picks the short one. They tell him to be discreet and break it to her gently.

"No problem," Anderson says. So, he drives over to the Smith house and knocks on the door. The wife answers.

"Your husband just lost $500 playing cards," he tells her.

She screams in annoyance and says, "Tell him to drop dead!"

Anderson replies, "Okay. I'll tell him."

Philandering

Wise old Ben Franklin was probably not the first to observe that, "Where there is marriage without love, there will be love without marriage." Two questions arise. First, has philandering become more prevalent now than when Ben wrote that in the 1700s in his Poor Richards Almanac? Or is it simply because our media is faster, more diverse, and technically superior to his limited almanac circulation, spreading sordid tales to the masses more efficiently. Are we simply better informed or is the practice itself that much more pervasive today? I have not seen any data making a moral comparison between the two times in American history. Perhaps it is simply that sleaze is more in demand, so the media (magazines, TV, movies) respond with more stories, more examples for consumption, giving the impression at least that everybody's doin' it!

Compulsive behavior in a man begins with his wandering eye. This transfers to his brain which conjures up delectable pleasantries while totally ignoring possible future adverse consequences. If he is fortunate enough to remember that he doesn't have enough blood to operate both his brain and his penis, he will nip the urge quickly before his blood supply heads south. If not, he enters the danger zone, the results of which can be disastrous and literally life threatening.

According to Bits and Pieces, here are five rules for a happy life that Russell J. Jackson had inscribed on his tombstone, in Logan, Utah. He died not knowing he would someday win "The Coolest Headstone Contest." Inscribed on his marker were the following five admonitions.

"It's important to have a woman who helps at home,

cooks, cleans up, and has a job.

It's important to have a woman who can make you laugh.

It's important to have a woman who you can trust and doesn't lie to you.

It's important to have a woman who is good in bed and likes to be with you.

It is very, very important that these four women do not know each other, or you could end up dead, like me!"

On Being Completed

Beautiful Hungarian-born movie sex symbol Zsa Zsa Gabor had six husbands in her glamorous Hollywood life. I think she appeared on the Johnny Carson Show several times and was not only gorgeous but entertaining, saying funny and clever things. Often it has been said that a man is not complete until he is married with family. Zsa Zsa put a slight twist on that traditional theme by saying,

> *A man in love is incomplete until he is married.*
> *Then, he's finished.*

I will end this chapter with a *Readers Digest* story about linguistics that fits in perfectly now following Zsa Zsa. No English dictionary has been able to adequately explain the difference between these two words, COMPLETE or FINISHED. In a recent linguistics competition held in London and attended by supposedly the best and brightest in the world, Samdar Balgobin, a Guyanese man was a clear winner, with a standing ovation which lasted for over five minutes.

The final question was: How do you explain the difference between the words COMPLETE and FINISHED in a way that is easy to understand? Some say there is no difference between these two words.

Here is the astute winning answer: When you marry the right woman, you are COMPLETE. When you marry the wrong woman, you are FINISHED. When the right one catches you with the wrong one, you are COMPLETELY FINISHED!!!" He won a trip around the world and a case of 25-year-old Scotch.

Favorite Love Songs

Today's generation seems unfamiliar with the master composers and performers of previous decades — the depression years of the '30's, the anxious war years of the '40's, and the happy days' time of the '50's. What follows are sixteen reminders of a more romantic time — of beautiful melodies coupled with sentimental lyrics. Here are some of my favorites.

For a romantic evening, I suggest you sit by the fire and enjoy some of these classic love songs:

- *When I Fall in Love*
- *Through the Eyes of Love* (Theme from the movie Ice Castles)
- *Together*
- *The Things We Did Last Summer*
- *Dear Heart*
- *As Time Goes By*
- *Days of Wine and Roses*
- *You Light Up My Life*
- *Through the Years*
- *Blue Moon*
- *Stardust*

- *Night and Day*
- *These Foolish Things*
- *I'll Be Seeing You*
- *We'll Meet Again*
- *September Song*

and lastly *True Love* by Cole Porter, which is my favorite. It was the theme song in the movie *HIGH SOCIETY* in 1958 sung by Bing Crosby and Grace Kelly (she later became the Princess of Monaco).

True Love

Sun tanned, windblown
Honeymooners at last alone
Feeling far above par
Oh, how lucky we are
While I give to you and you give to me
True love, true love
So on and on it will always be,
True love, true love
For you and I have a guardian angel
On high, with nothing to do,
But to give to you and to give to me
love forever true

CHAPTER FOUR

The 2nd Most Important Choice

Choosing to Improve Yourself

Anyone who owns a house must be committed to endlessly fixing up the place. This commitment is not only to make it a home the way you want it, but to also have it retain, or — better still — increase, its investment value.

I had a neighbor where we lived in Collegeville, Pennsylvania, who classified all things household into three categories. He said he was either maintaining the property, advancing the property, or, if he did nothing, the property was regressing. Things like cutting the grass, painting, and repairing a stone wall all fell into the category of maintaining. However, if he had cut down brush and replaced the area by planting grass, that would be advancing. In like manner, if you were painting a newly built garden shed, that too would be advancing, as would be building a new stone wall where there was none before.

The never-ending chores of home ownership pale in comparison to the greater challenge of maintaining and advancing one's own self. What you do or don't do is a choice. You can choose to just float along in life carried by whatever circumstances come your way. The reality, however, is that it is impossible to maintain a static position, or an unchanging stature, in life because TIME GOES BY, and you are getting older. When time enters life's equation, you are either getting better or you are getting worse. Life is all about creating momentum because time doesn't stand still. You are either moving forward or backward.

As you age beyond youthfulness, chances are that you are not going to get healthier, more motivated, nor have more energy without putting the effort into advancing through healthy lifestyle choices and habits. You've got an age window in which to advance. You have to push yourself forward while you are able and fit in order to physically accomplish your goals and finish the race strong. George Elliott has said, "It's never too late to be who you might have been." Or, as David Jeremiah says, "If you're not dead, you're not done!"

So, the choice becomes twofold: either one must make a conscious decision to get better or allow oneself to get worse! We have choices. We are not like a peanut shell floating on the stream of life, subject to every current and eddy with no control over our circumstances and destiny. Football great Roger Staubach said it best,

> Winning isn't getting ahead of others. It's getting ahead of yourself.

A newly planted garden must be watered, weeded, fertilized, and nurtured or it will turn into an overgrown jungle or barren wasteland. In like manner, to get better we must cultivate our mind and body. Neither develops overnight. Growth is a process which should be continuous, ongoing, long drawn out, and never ending. Stephen Covey, author of the best-selling book *The 7 Habits of Highly Effective People*, said, "Be patient with yourself. Self-growth is tender: it's holy ground. There is no greater investment."

Are You Teachable?

My wife, Molly, and I spent several years counseling a bright young man whose life was negatively impacted by his compulsive, addictive behavior. He lost friends, got thrown out of graduate school, was told not to pursue a career in the ministry, was fired from multiple jobs, and wasted what should have been a decade of productive years in his life. This young man only wanted encouragement not honest feedback. He wasn't that interested in instruction, and he definitely did not want correction! Because of this, we tried to encourage him at every opportunity, both through emails and face-to-face meetings, for anything he did well. Ephesians 4:29 tells us, "Let everything you say be good and helpful so that your words will be an encouragement to those who hear them."

However, true feedback must be transparent and honest, and a mentor's encouragement of the protégé must always be tempered with necessary instruction and correction in the best interest of progress. This young man showed that he was unteachable. He didn't listen well to teaching and didn't want to hear constructive criticism. He didn't want to confront the truth. He was wise in his own eyes and would only hear what he wanted to hear. A mentor will always tell the protégé the truth, not just those things the protégé wants to hear. And then, it is up to the protégé to receive it or not.

That young man was on a hamster wheel, expending

boundless energy going round and round, yet going nowhere. If a person initiates compulsive behavior without thinking about where that behavior will lead or what the next step is, they may be shocked by where it takes them. Jail is sometimes a possibility. In terms of self-discipline, use this simple criterion: If you wouldn't tell your mother or grandmother about it, just don't do it! And always listen to those who are pouring into you. Their words may be temporarily hurtful, but it can save you a lifetime of harm.

You Are Who You Say You Are

If you are a Peter Sellers fan, as I am, you may recall that in the movie *The Pink Panther Strikes Again*, former Chief Inspector Dreyfus was under treatment in an asylum for the mentally bewildered because Inspector Clouseau, Peter Sellers' character, drove him crazy. He was instructed to keep repeating the words, "Every day, in every way, I'm getting better and better." We have learned that by repeating such positive statements, we are reprogramming ourselves.

Maxwell Maltz, author of *Psycho Cybernetics*, tells us that our subconscious brain accepts, believes, and then adopts these repetitions. Self-speak can be positive or negative and influences our attitude accordingly. Since perhaps, most people could use a larger dose of enthusiasm, take the example of what is taught during the basic Dale Carnegie self-improvement course. During one of the sessions, students are taught to say the following, over and over with increasing enthusiasm:

> *Think enthusiastic and you'll act enthusiastic.*
> *Act enthusiastic and you'll be enthusiastic!*

Leonard Cohen said it this way, "Act the way you'd like to be and soon you'll be the way you act." Nothing is wrong with that little trick of self-deception in advancing your path of self-improvement, teasing yourself to get better. The same idea is incorporated with the use and repetition of positive affirmations. According to author Maxwell Maltz, such positive thoughts are implanted in your subconscious brain where they eventually become beliefs.

Dexter always taught that, "We get older automatically, but we have to work at getting better." He also said, "We get better by building on our strengths and talents, learning to delegate our weaknesses." Someone once said, "You don't have to be sick to get better!"

Perhaps most of us, in facing ourselves, find that we waffle between our confident desire to improve and our reluctance and/or lack of confidence to launch forth. Carl Sandburg once captured this feeling with the following self-appraisal, "There is an eagle in me that wants to soar, and there is a hippopotamus in me that wants to wallow in the mud." As we vacillate between our two selves, keep in mind what Longfellow observed, "We judge ourselves by what we think we are capable of doing, but others judge us by what we have already done."

Process

You have heard the expression, "Two heads are better than one." In making essential choices, this is most certainly true. Similarly, the timeless carpenters' adage says, "Measure twice. Cut once."

We recently moved into a new house on five wooded acres on a gentle slope to a stream. We were putting in a stone retaining wall for a patio area and fencing in the backyard so we could just let our dogs out, and they would be contained. We also wanted the fence to inhibit future visits from the black bear we saw walking across our front yard during one of our first evenings in residence. I had envisioned a way for the fence to go over the wall so the dogs could not use it to jump over and escape. I explained my plan to my daughter Carolyn, who is innovative and a good problem solver. She observed, thought for a minute, and made a suggestion. Her idea was to simply move the fence several feet to the left where it would not have the complications of going over the wall. This was a much simpler and better plan. I was left asking myself: now why didn't I think of that? I had simply locked in on the first idea that occurred to me. The benefit of a second opinion is that it may present a simpler or better way. Yes, indeed, "Two heads are better than one!"

There's a Reason We Have Two Ears and One Mouth

This leads me to mention the essential mental attitude of being teachable and pursuing the process of mentorship when considering each of the crucial choices that come along in life. A thoughtful *Dexterism* about seeking advice went like this: "Only take the advice of those who stand to benefit from your success." Simple enough to understand. If a person stands to benefit from your success, they will give you the best advice they can because it is mutually beneficial. They have a stake in the outcome. In such a relationship, to give less than the best counsel would be counterproductive for all concerned. Seeking or, worse yet, taking advice from an unknown source, or someone with an axe to grind, or the man on the street, or the biased news media, would be foolish indeed.

Seek and take the advice of those who have been successful or living the lifestyle you want to emulate. In one of his worthy "Tip of The Week" emails, author and leadership development expert Robert Rohm retells a familiar story about how to make good choices and decisions. A young man asked an older gentleman how he became so successful. The older man responded, "By making good decisions." The young man then asked, "How did you learn to make good decisions?" The older man replied, "By making bad decisions."

Yes, experience is the best teacher, but it can also be the most expensive. Learning from the mistakes and wisdom of others is a shortcut. I once had a barber and a dentist, both of whom loved to talk and give advice and had a captive audience pinned down in a chair. In the dentist's case, patients could not reply 95 percent of the time. This never developed into a conversation but instead was a monologue. Almost everyone loves to be asked for advice and will readily give it. However, without a relationship, expertise, or credibility, of what value is the advice one would get? I might add that unsolicited advice, no matter how well-intended, is often ignored or rejected with annoyance.

In our youth, we start out with dreams and plans for our future. To make a point, I heard motivational speaker Les Brown, at a Yager business conference, tell a story of an old man near the end of his days in a hospital bed. He wakes up from dozing to find a crowd in his room surrounding his bed. They look concerned and sad. The old man speaks weakly and says, "Y'all must be my friends from long ago who have come to say goodbye. Thank you."

Stepping up to greet the old man, grasping his hand tenderly is a figure who says, "You are right, we are some of your best and oldest friends. However, long ago you left us. We are the unfulfilled promises and dreams of your youth you once were excited about but never initiated. We are the special talents you were given but never tried or developed. We are the special gifts you never learned about yourself. Old man, we have not come to comfort you but rather to die with you." Oh, how sad is a life unfulfilled!

Whether you focus on your strengths or your weaknesses, or whether you choose to soar or wallow, is to exercise your second most important choice in life. As Shakespeare wrote, "To be or not to be? That is the question." I have arbitrarily listed this choice as second in importance because without making a committed choice to improve yourself, all the other important choices you make will be adversely affected!

Just as I am

Once or twice in my life, I have overheard someone say, "Well, that's just the way I am. Love me or leave me." Wrong attitude. That person, if they don't become teachable, change their ways, and get better, will be doomed to mediocrity at best.

There is an old hymn called "Just As I Am, Thine Own to Be" by Marianne Hearn. The fourth verse says:
> Just as I am, young, strong, and free,
> to be the best that I can be

For truth, and righteousness, and Thee,
Lord of my life, I come.

The Lord accepts us as we are and begins a work in progress. Even as we may strive to get better, we all will fall short of perfection. Unlike the Lord, other humans may not always be so kind or patient with us when we fall short, demonstrating our imperfections.

Several years ago, an old friend, Ken, who I have known since fifth grade, and I were driving from the Carolinas to Dayton, Ohio, to visit the Air Force Museum. We graduated from high school together and have stayed in touch with each other over the years. He is a very smart guy and became an aeronautical engineer after serving in the Air Force. His wife had recently passed away so I thought it would be good for us to take this trip to explore an area of our mutual interest, the history of military aviation. While I was driving, I brought up the four personality categories and how important the concept was in understanding oneself and others. He had never heard of such a thing and asked if I was making this up. So, just in case, if you too, dear reader, are one of those to yet be introduced to the 4 basic temperaments, allow me to offer a crash course, to at least whet your appetite.

The Four Temperaments

This personality assessment recognizes that we are all born with certain inborn traits. The theory states that these inborn traits are typically found in one of four distinct personality types, or models of human behavior. Each of us has one type that is most dominant and one of secondary dominance. It was first conceived in Ancient Greece by Socrates, and in more recent times, it has been advanced by personal development experts such as Tim LaHaye, Florence Littauer, Robert Rohm, and others. Many now refer to these four temperaments as the DISC personality assessment. Since there are whole books written on the subject, I will keep my mention as brief and simple as I dare.

First, there is the Choleric or D personality. The "D" stands for Dominance. This is the high achieving, leader-type person who wants and likes control. They live by the motto, "Take charge!" But they can sometimes be blunt, even insensitive, and are often convinced that they are right. It has been suggested that one of the things that causes polarization and gridlock in Washington is that too many of our elected officials are of this personality type. They all think they are right and theirs is the only way to go. This makes partisan politics more partisan.

As I mentioned earlier, women get more "choleric" with the responsibilities of wifehood and, particularly, motherhood when they have to take charge making many decisions. This I have noticed in Molly as she adjusted from her inborn primary trait of phlegmatic to become more choleric in nature.

Our eldest daughter Carolyn is a take-charge person. She has held several jobs during her lifetime and has performed each in an outstanding way, perhaps outshining her superiors to such a degree as to not have received the appreciation and recognition she deserved. In our recent move, she was an invaluable help managing many of the details that were essential, especially during a two-week period while Molly and I were out of state. She and I both have this as our dominant personality. On rare occasions, we clash. She is a strong, smart Christian and is aware of these personality types. As long as a choleric person remembers to manage their tendency to take over things, and not let bossiness get out of control, they are less likely to run over people.

Dexter taught that, "Our greatest strength is our greatest weakness." We are most successful using and relying on our strengths. However, our greatest strengths become our greatest weakness if undisciplined, out of control, and/or are unmanaged. Without discipline, our greatest strength may become too much of a good thing. At such times, the choleric person risks offending and alienating other people.

The attribute of being smart, in this example, means understanding yourself and your nature. Emerson (Ralph Waldo that is) said, "Know thyself," and Shakespeare wrote, "To thine own self be true." That, along with a desire to get along, coupled with the mellowing effect of aging, should tone down more extreme emotional responses to any conflicts. As noted in a previous chapter, love leads to understanding and understanding leads to love. The catalyst is communication. As long as two people are willing to communicate, they can solve problems and moderate differences. If communication is cut off, leaving issues unresolved, ill feelings will linger like a growing cancer in a relationship.

Second, there is the Melancholy or C personality, who is detail-oriented, analytical, neat, and well-ordered. The "C" stands for Compliance or Conscientiousness. Often, they have superior spatial relations and are gifted artistically and creatively. However, they can get bogged down in the details of life to a point where, in the extreme, they have difficulty loosening up and going with the flow. This is my and Molly's secondary characteristic. It is not surprising then, that this is a type that shows up in each of our children to varying degrees.

In my forties, before becoming aware of these inborn personalities, a new acquaintance described me as being austere. I had heard that word but was not totally sure of its meaning. I looked it up and found the definition: "stern, harsh, morally strict, plain." I was shocked to be perceived that way in a first impression. I didn't think of myself that way, and I didn't want to fit that description in the minds of others. I resolved immediately to change that perception, to get better, to be more outgoing at first, to smile more, to learn some jokes, and to adapt to being more sanguine-like, which I like to think I have done successfully.

Third, the Sanguine or I individual is expressive, the fun-loving, popular, life of the party, who generally loves people and whom, in turn, people love. It is easy to see why "I" stands for Influence. They are not into details much and in a lifetime will misplace their car keys more than most. They sometimes come across as being too nice to be real, maybe even perceived as superficial. We have no sanguine children, only a few sanguine grandchildren and two wives that have married into our family. Both of them have married strong melancholies. See, once again, opposites attract.

Finally, there is the Phlegmatic individual or S type. The "S" stands for Steadiness. This is Molly's primary inborn temperament although modified by motherhood as mentioned above. A phlegmatic is soft-spoken, laid-back, mild-mannered, and someone who generally doesn't ruffle feathers. They wear well, but they also can be stubborn and unteachable. While neither stubborn nor unteachable, our third daughter Holly has this as her dominant trait as well. She is not only one of the hardest workers in our family, but she has a servant's heart, can endure frustration, is very adaptable, is most compassionate, and is a joy to have around.

My "melancholy," very artistically talented, and creative son has this as his secondary trait. He functions well as a team player, just as he did as the co-captain of his high school basketball team. There, his spatial relations helped him to be one of the best three-point shooters in the state and whose record stood for decades at his high school. Those same talents help him today as a graphic artist. Wherever he is employed, he is very highly regarded.

There is no best personality. None is superior to the others, and they have nothing to do with intelligence. Each personality has its own strengths and weaknesses. Understanding these four types is a giant step forward in self-awareness, and also in becoming better able to work with other people. Understanding these personality types is a critical component in improving oneself. My wife Molly has often said, "I wish I had known about these personality types when our children were little."

If you are not familiar with this subject matter and want to know more, I suggest that you check out Personality Insights and the work of Dr. Robert Rohm. He has written several books on the topic and is a most entertaining speaker. He conducts excellent workshops and has a variety of related instructional materials available. He is, in my opinion, the most informed and dynamic authority in the field. I like him.

I trust him. I think you will too.

So, you are what you are, with certain inborn temperaments and specific God-given talents. Most of those attributes you have to discover yourself, which means being open to trying new things. Orison Swett Marden, founder of Success Magazine, said, "There are powers inside of you which, if you could discover and use, would make of you everything you ever dreamed or imagined you could become." You are a work in progress that will never achieve perfection and not be completed until the day you die. That requires that you strive to get better. Here is a country western song that I first heard performed by a singing group during the 70s at Heritage USA, near Pineville, North Carolina. The words are,

> Some folks are gettin' caught up with the movie stars
> and what they're watchin' on TV.
> Some are gettin' caught up with the latest fads.
> But it really doesn't matter to me.
> You see I don't give a rip about the latest.
> Or what the anchor man has to say.
> I've got my eye on makin' me the greatest.
> And I'm gettin' better every day.

You Are Who You Think You Are

I heard a long time ago that your image of yourself shapes so many other aspects of your life, so that, I am not necessarily what I think I am. Nor am I what others think I am. I am what I think others think I am! Dr. Joyce Brothers said that "Our self-concept is the core of our personality. It's no exaggeration to say that a strong positive self-image is the best possible preparation for success in life."

There is no doubt that tennis great John McEnroe had a

healthy self-image. Because of his combination of confidence and aggressive athletic ability he was known for his great, artistic play and world-class competitiveness. He was also known for his quick temper and oversized ego. His confidence level is on display with the following two quotations:

"My greatest strength is that I have no weaknesses."

"The older I get, the greater I was."

My notes from a graduate psychology class remind me of what self-love is and what it is not. Self-love is not arrogance, narcissism, self-glorification, nor self-will. Self-love is a sense of self-worth, an emotion of self-respect, being trusted, knowing you are wanted, giving your love to someone who needs it, and being true to your highest ideals.

Walmart founder Sam Walton echoes that thought by saying, "If people believe in themselves, it's amazing what they can accomplish." I think I may have mentioned the phenomenon before, that most people overestimate others and underestimate themselves. Interestingly enough, I think there is one self-image that unites all human beings, regardless of age, gender, religion, race, nationality, or temperament. That is, we all seem to believe we are above-average drivers. Ha!

One of my favorite comedians of the '70's and 80's was Rodney Dangerfield, who always complained, as part of his routine, that he never got any respect. He said on the Johnny Carson show that, "Once I told my old man, nobody likes me. My father said, 'Don't say that. Not everybody's met you yet.'"

Yes, you are what you are, but you are not expected to stay that way. An old English proverb states that you may find the worst enemy or best friend in yourself. You should say, in your self-talk, "I'm better than I used to be. I'm better than I was yesterday. Hopefully I'm not as good as I'm going to be tomorrow." That's the right attitude needed for self-improvement. After all, you are engaged in an ongoing journey of discovery called life. The biggest challenge you will face is that of self-discovery, improvement, and management. Chinese philosopher Lao-Tzu said, "He who conquered others is strong: He who conquered himself is mighty." Not long ago I saw the following wisdom on a plaque in a gift shop:

Knowing others is intelligence

Knowing yourself is true wisdom

Mastering others is strength

Mastering yourself is true power

In Dexter Yager's book, *Pursuit*, he wrote, "The door to self-improvement opens from the inside." Ralph Waldo Emerson said, "The only person you are destined to become is the person you decide to be." That is an interesting thought. Did it ever occur to you that you can actually choose the person you want to be? Just like you can choose your future.

One of the most popular authors of American history, particularly on the subject of cowboys and the westward movement across our country, has been Louis L'Amour. I found his saga of the multi-generational Sackett family especially captivating. Louis L'Amour was speaking about taking charge of your life when he said the following:

"Up to a point a man's life is shaped by environment, heredity, and movements and changes in the world around him: then there comes a time when it lies within his grasp to shape the clay of his life into the sort of thing he wishes to be... Everyone has it within his power to say, THIS I am today, THAT I shall be tomorrow."

Even though everyone knows there are only Ten Biblical Commandments, an eleventh commandment has been suggested: "Thou shalt not kid thyself." We need frequent checks along the road of life to ensure we are on the right path, doing the right things, and using our God-given talents, in order to end up in the right place, where we choose to be. Think of your life's journey this way. Who you are is God's gift to you. Who you become is your gift back to God. The whole matter is in your hands. You choose!

The Journey

There are only three time periods in your life - the past, the present, and the future. Fulton Oursler, author of the exceptional book, The Greatest Story Ever Told, wrote, "Many of us crucify ourselves between two thieves- regret for the past and fear of the future." Genius Albert Einstein offers this perspective, "Learn from yesterday, live for today, hope for tomorrow." According to Lao Tzu, "If you are depressed, you are living in the past. If you are anxious, you are living in the future. If you are at peace, you are living in the present." Author and motivational speaker, Jim Stovall speaking to a Yager business conference said it this way, "Yesterday is history. Tomorrow is a mystery. Today is a gift."

The PAST is over and done! There is no instant replay, as there is on Monday night football. Whatever has been stands firm in the sands of time and cannot be changed. The victories, the defeats, the errors of omission, and the errors of commission are there for all to see in the history book of your life. What's done is done. We can only go forward from here. Jessica Long is one of America's most decorated Olympians from the Paralympic Games. She put things in the proper perspective when she said, "If you can get excited about your future, your past won't matter."

The FUTURE hasn't come yet. So, the only time we can immediately impact is NOW! What we do today cannot alter the past, but it may likely affect the future. That makes today really important. Noted author on leadership, John Maxwell said that we exaggerate yesterday, we overestimate tomorrow, and we underestimate today.

The Scripture tells us in Matthew 6:33-34,

> But seek first the kingdom of God and His righ-
> teousness, and all these things shall be added to
> you. Therefore, do not worry about tomorrow, for
> tomorrow will worry about it's own trouble.

That's right. Don't worry about tomorrow, do something about today. We need to make each day count for something, as it is the only path for bringing about the future we want. Now, I don't want to go too fast here and lose you, because this concept is so important to understand. Many people don't think about it. They may give more thought to planning a trip or a party, or who gets what for Christmas, than they seriously plan their own future. They drift into their future guided mostly by circumstance.

Life's Roundabouts

I have visited Europe many times. The first time was while I was in the Army, on a Liberty ship, a WWII vintage troop transport. On the other successive trips, we often flew into

London's Heathrow airport. Several times we rented a car so we could take some time and see the British countryside. My Uncle Bill, with his Scottish background and enthusiasm, planted this seed in my young brain, "Roland, sometime in your life you must cover the grand island of Great Britain from John O'Groats at the northeast tip of Scotland to Lands End at the southwest tip of Cornwall, England." We have done that. We've seen the sights from Inverness and Loch Ness to the Isle of Skye, to Edinburgh, Sterling, Winchester, and Windsor Castles, to Bath, Stonehenge, the British Museum, the Imperial War Museum, the London Eye, Hadrian's Wall and cruised the Thames River.

Many times, during our challenge of driving on the "wrong" side of the road, we would come to a traffic circle- a roundabout as they call them- which seemed overly prevalent in Britain. Good thing, though, as circling about one gave us Americans a chance to think about where we were going. First, on coming upon such a circle, it is essential to remember to turn left into the circle instead of to the right as we would do here. When in heavy traffic, it was easy just to follow the car in front of us. We forgot once and made the mistake of turning right, head on into the oncoming traffic. The other cars swerved or stopped, and we corrected without playing crinkle fender with anybody. One British driver just made a face, while another shouted a few cuss words followed by, "Bloody American!" Couldn't blame him. We shrugged with guilt, raised an eyebrow, and waved back. At least he didn't give us "the bird" as a rude American might do.

The point of the roundabout story is that when we didn't know which of the alternative roads out of the circle to take, we just continued round and round until we figured out which way to go. Sometimes making life's choices, about which way to go, is similar. Which of the alternatives is our road to success? While pondering that question, you just may have to go round and round spinning your wheels and going nowhere for a while, until you figure out the best direction. Christians refer to this as "waiting on the Lord." If you don't wait, that impatient mistake often costs in terms of both time and money. Circling patiently is better than hurriedly making the wrong choice and having to back track. As the saying goes,

> *Patience is a virtue.*
> *Possess it if you can.*
> *Seldom found in women.*
> *And never found in man!*

Futurists tell us that each of us face hundreds of future possibilities, yet we will end up with only one future, our future. Well, which one will it be? Which future, out of the many possibilities, will you end up with? Do you want to take a chance on a future that circumstance brings? A BIG EMPHATIC NO! You want to choose your future in advance. Once done, today's choices become vastly easier because you have identified where you want to go.

Too many people plod along day to day, in the present, without much thought about where they're going. It was probably one of the great philosophers who first said it (Aristotle, Ben Franklin, Abraham Lincoln, Winston Churchill, Yogi Berra, Pogo, or maybe Charlie Brown), "If you don't know where you are going, you will likely end up somewhere else!"

The PRESENT is the only time we can immediately impact,

so seize the day! Choose a path. What is the ultimate destination of your chosen path? In order to make your PRESENT days productive, and actually take you in the direction you wish to go, you must first choose your FUTURE in advance, out of those many possibilities. Once you decide on the future you want, then that makes it much easier to know what to do each day to take you most expeditiously toward your destiny!

Most of us learn in tenth grade geometry (the only math course in which I got an A) the theorem that states, "The shortest distance between two points is a straight line." The same is true in life. We don't want any distracting, delaying, inconvenient detours along your road to success. The caterpillar in Alice in Wonderland wisely said, "If you don't know where you are going, it really doesn't matter which road you take."

Dream Big or Not at All

Most people's future is wrapped around their dreams and goals. We only get one shot at life, one pass through this world. What do you want out of the life you have been given? It is hard for me to imagine, in a free country such as ours, that there are among us those who are plodders and not dreamers. There are those who are unmotivated, unteachable, not open to opportunity, and who are unwilling to move past mediocrity. Worse yet are those who adopt a victim mentality as opposed to striving. Dreams should be what drives us. They are the fuel for our fire. Be motivated, ambitious, and teachable! Seek change. Be willing to grow. If you don't try new things, you may never find out what you're good at! Be bolder in becoming.

Rich DeVos, co-founder of the Amway Corporation, billionaire, and once owner of the Orlando Magic professional basketball team, was once asked, "What is the main difference between the wealthy and the poor, between the haves and the have nots?" Perhaps many people would have answered the obvious in terms of material things. The rich have more, bigger, and better stuff — houses, cars, yachts, etc. Rich answered, "The big difference is the way they think. All those material things are outcomes and the manifestations of their thought process."

Dreams, however, cannot stand alone or they become vague wisps of obscurity and fade into nothingness without turning their abstraction into goals. Those who fail to make that transition simply say goodbye to their dreams. They become a faded pipe dream or just a pie in the sky. Dreams are nothing more than a vague imagination unless they are transitioned into goals. Three things distinguish goals from dreams.

First, dreams are most often vague and ill defined, whereas goals are SPECIFIC! Dreams say I want to have a nice car, or I want to live in a nice house someday. Goals spell out in specific terms make, model, color, and accessories on a car. Likewise, with a home, goals spell out the specifics of size, style, location, and features. The more specific you get the better, because the more concrete the goal the more likely it is to be attained.

Second, dreams are "maybe someday," unlike goals, which must have a specific TIME FRAME by which to be accomplished, therefore producing a sense of urgency. Dreams may come floating in someday, but goals must be pursued consistently and persistently.

Third, dreams are based on hope, unlike goals which require a PLAN for accomplishment. As pastor and author Robert Schuler said, "Inch by inch, life's a cinch. Yard by yard, life is hard." Most achievers accomplish their goals the old-fashioned way, step by step. Very few win the lottery, strike oil in the backyard, marry wealth, or through other means become an overnight success, in one fell-swoop.

Success is a process that requires a plan. Author Glen Bland defined success as "the progressive realization of a pre-determined worthwhile goal." Almost all successful people first must go through the GRIT and GRIND before they get to the GLORY!

To put this discussion of dreams and goals in perspective, I will insert some words of wisdom from business leader and life coach Rick Setzer, in an outstanding talk I heard him give about passion and purpose. He explained that passion is something we admire in people. You don't get passion from goals. It comes from having a purpose. A purpose is emotional. We are analytical and methodical in accomplishing goals, but our purpose deals with our "calling in life." It is normally centered around people not things. Things like freedom, loving someone, spirituality, or making a positive difference in the world.

Goal Getters

To accomplish your purpose, you must have a vehicle with which to do it. If your vehicle is dented, has a bad engine, looks horrible and is not capable of making the trip, you'll give up on your purpose. Your purpose then becomes a pipe dream. For Rick and several others mentioned in this book, the worthy vehicle that they drove to fulfillment, financial success, and an outstanding lifestyle was found in serving others. That meant being entrepreneurs, leading, mentoring, and going to work for others, setting them up in their own business, and helping them to be successful. A true win–win situation.

The objective or goal is to win the game, whether it be the game of life or football. From one, we can learn principles to apply to the other. Every football coach prepares a game plan to be employed against the next opponent. This plan is based on scouting reports and what is known about the opposing team, their record against who they played, strengths and weaknesses, all designed to defeat them and win the game. If, however, at halftime the coach finds himself behind by three touchdowns, he better adjust, scrap the initial plan, and come up with a modified approach before it's too late. Or he will face defeat.

The same is true in life. If you are seemingly stuck on a hamster wheel, just going round and round expending effort but going nowhere fast, it may be time to assess what is and isn't working for you and create a different plan to get to the future you want.

At age 42, I was a tenured professor at a major state university. I was President–elect of my state professional association. I made presentations at our national convention and published in professional journals. I received superior reviews from students. I taught a course over television that went out to a half dozen regional campuses. In short, I was a professional success.

However, I was unhappy, overworked, stressed out, and underpaid. I was putting in 70 hours a week on the job, painting and fixing up the house we had bought, struggling to raise four children and two large dogs, while coping with university politics as thick as a storm cloud – all requiring responsibilities impinging on my life. I'm sure I must have been grumpy and stressed too, with which Molly had to deal. I didn't think I wanted to go through the rest of life this way. I just had to do something more or something different!

Shazam! Along came the Amway business from someone we didn't even know. We were a referral. The timing couldn't have been better. Had it come along earlier, I probably would have turned up my nose, as we had a certain degree of status and acceptance because of my position and Molly's historical family. We lived in a house we were fixing up in a nice neighborhood, but I had to face the reality that, despite how things appeared on the outside, we were one paycheck away from bankruptcy. To reach our goal of a balanced, peaceful life, we recognized we would have to choose a focused, out of balance, even more frenzied life for a while in order to exit the hamster wheel.

Fortunately, we understood delayed gratification and were willing to put work before play, investment before reward, sacrifice before pleasure. So, for several years I pushed myself, burned the midnight oil, and slept fast. We used to joke that, when forced to push it, one could sleep twice as fast by putting carbon paper under your pillow. In that way, four hours could become eight hours of sleep. Sometimes, "you just gotta suck it up and do whatcha gotta do!" Someone once said, the day will happen whether you get up or not.

Two Ways to Go

I have ranked the choice of improving and conquering one-self second because it forms a foundation upon which all other choices depend. In contemplating self-improvement, these are the two choices one faces: do nothing, get bitter, get better. What's the matter, can't you count? That's three! No, it boils down to just two. If you do nothing, the result invariably ends unsatisfactorily, and you end up bitter as life passes you by and opportunities are missed.

Captain Wood at OCS said to us, "An officer needs to be decisive. Never tell a real man to 'take care.' You tell a real man to 'take charge!'" Be bold! He said, "Do something, even if it ends up you were wrong." But do it decisively. Like the baseball umpire declares, you are either safe or you're out—there is no in-between. Shout it out loud and be clear with emphatic gestures. Take charge of your life. Make the conscious choice to get better. Don't just talk about it, DO IT!

Develop Healthy Habits

What follows is not meant to put down anyone who may be overweight but rather to caution them as to the very real dangers in carrying excess weight into middle age. I'd encourage them to do something about their condition before it becomes a severe health problem. The excuse given most frequently by an overweight person is, "It's in my genes. I can't help it." Partially true. Certainly, genes may cause a tendency towards weight gain. If you discover that you are genetically predisposed to weight gain, take action immediately to manage it before it gets out of hand. Don't take the easy path and just give into it. Don't accept it as a done deal and a foregone conclusion you can't do anything about. Don't surrender to it. Like so many things, as I have pointed out throughout this book, it is your choice. Coach Lou Holtz said, "Self-discipline is an individual's greatest asset." Put it to work. Take charge! Don't become a victim.

This is a story, of a once big (300 pounder), powerful, strong, athletic football lineman who started for a Division I university up north. His transition in health and weight gain has been replicated by many other linemen over the years and throughout the country. When a man weighs that much during his active playing days and has formed a habit of eating large quantities of food to maintain his needed bulk, look out!

Heart disease, high blood pressure, lethargy, joint and mobility problems, and Type 2 Diabetes are lurking in wait. Too many retired football players have become overweight and incurred health problems, which for some, have led to premature death. The activity comes to an end, but the eating habits and weight gain often continue unless radical changes are made. This man "blimped up" to a point where he became lethargic, irresponsible, and depressed. He wouldn't work and developed serious mobility problems, not to mention becoming selfish and disagreeable, as he aged and became more sedentary.

He had two sons who followed in his footsteps to also become good eaters and big heavy football lineman. Both had, in their genes, a propensity for weight gain. One son, now in his mid-thirties, has been talking about losing weight for over two decades. If anything, he continues to get heavier. He is smart, has a pleasing personality, has a handsome face, is caring and dependable. However, he is not just heavy. He is grossly overweight, unhealthily so, to the point of obesity. His heavy appearance detracts from the first impression he makes, which in turn places limits on some job opportunities, not to mention diminishing romantic possibilities. He could be good looking if he would only trim down. It would significantly change his life for the better in every way. I pray for him every day that he will discipline himself and conquer himself before it is too late!

Many years ago, we were working with a team which included a very overweight couple. They suffered from various health problems commonly associated with obesity. They had a daughter in her 20s, a lovely woman with a pleasant voice and a pleasing manner, who also struggled with her weight.

One evening, the three of them attended a business meeting which was so well attended we had to resort to setting out folding chairs. As everyone was settling into their seats, there was a loud crash in the back of the room. We all looked around to find the source of the commotion, quickly discovering that the young woman had fallen as the folding chair had collapsed beneath her. She lay sprawled on the floor, awkwardly trying to get up. After she was helped to her feet, she and her parents hurriedly left the meeting, the tears of embarrassment still fresh in her eyes. Witnessing such a painful moment for that young woman has remained with me all these years. I felt such empathy for her. For an obese person, the first impression they make is so often dominated by their size.

I am reminded of an expression I first heard back in the sixties, "Your appearance speaks so loudly, I can't hear what you say." In other words, your looks are so dominant they obliterate the rest of your persona. This is true of obesity, as I have just illustrated, but also applies to how you present yourself in general. It is important to be on time, well-groomed, appropriately dressed for the occasion, and well-mannered. As the old expression cautions, "You never get a second chance to make a first impression."

Your choice to be developed goes beyond the intellectual or vocational. It also includes the physical. Take beauty as a standard. With Jacqueline Smith or Elizabeth Taylor, their beautiful faces exceeded all else about them. With Pamela Anderson and Marilyn Monroe, sex appeal was the dominant first impression. Sheer size overwhelms when meeting Shaquille O'Neill. Appearing so regal, upon sight, Queen Elizabeth immediately humbled the common man, without saying a word. In establishing or repelling relationships, some people cannot get past the impact of that first impression. We should all want to put our best foot forward.

Change or Die

What do you do when a family member gets themselves into a life debilitating and/or a life-threatening situation? It matters not whether it is alcohol, drugs, bad or dangerous friends, or even unhealthy obesity. Should the family ignore and overlook it, for fear of offending or upsetting, hoping it will go away or get better? Of course not. It is addiction because the person is unable to conquer and overcome it by themselves. Is it somehow unloving or uncaring to confront, communicate, and clarify the problem and to try to help? No again. The opposite would be true. The addict needs help!

The first step in solving a problem is to recognize it. Admit it. Confront it. Then mobilize a plan to solve it. It should be readily apparent that whatever has been attempted, if anything, so far hasn't worked. Time is running out. With each passing day, the problem is only worsening.

Success is just a decision away. That is, a decision followed by the necessary commitment. You should know that there are three levels of commitment. The lowest level is, "I'll try." The second level is the Boy Scout level, "I'll do my best." Neither of those will get it done for you. You must employ the highest level of commitment, "I'll do whatever it takes!"

So, an important part of choosing to better yourself, which is the second most important choice, in your life, is to manage your body as well as your mind and attitude. Author and teacher, Sonya Parker shared, "Don't spend all your time trying to find yourself. Spend your time instead creating yourself into a person that you'll be proud of." Don't just be yourself, as long as you are at it, become somebody nicer.

For followers of Christ, Galatians 5:22-23 lists for us the character traits that should be evident in our lives: "The fruit of the spirit is love, joy, peace, long suffering, kindness, goodness, faithfulness, gentleness, and self-control." These are the qualities that reveal the mastery of oneself to then pursue our task at hand, which is to, "Let your light so shine before men, that they may see your good works, and glorify your Father which is in heaven" Matthew 5:16.

Means to an End

Everyone I have ever heard talk about success seems to agree that the most important ingredient in your success is YOU! "If it is to be, it is up to me!" As someone somewhat jokingly has said, "Everyone is self-made, but only the successful will admit it!" Thus, if you are not successful, it must be the fault of someone else, right? That kind of thinking means taking on a victim mentality instead of responsibility.

Philosopher Michael Bassey Johnson said, "You do not attain success when you associate with those in high places; it comes when you accept yourself and realize that only you can take yourself to where your heart truly lies." My mother always used to tell me, "You have to meet life's greatest challenges alone." While there may be many helpers along the way, there are just some things nobody else can do for you. No one else can experience your pain, nobody else can die for you, and nobody else can make you successful. Your strength must come from within.

I have told audiences far and wide that the elderly, when asked what would they do differently if they could live their life over, overwhelming answer that they would choose to be bolder! They would have tried more things, experimented, and been more adventurous.

Shakespeare wrote, "We know what we are, but know not what we may be." Most people do not sufficiently challenge themselves in life, daring to try the unknown. The great jurist Oliver Wendell Holmes, on observing this truth, commented, "Many people die with their music still in them."

So, what's a body to do? How about a step-by-step plan

to get better? OK! Here are some things you can do:

1. Seek mentorship in those areas of your life where you want to improve. Some people go through life trying all by themselves to re-invent the wheel. This may be due to ignorance, false pride, stubbornness, or even overconfidence. A mentor is someone who has achieved what you want, has demonstrated success, is where you would like to be, who knows what you would like to know, and is willing to impart those things to you. He does not need you. You need him! Mentorship requires pursuit!

2. In Kahlil Gibran's book, *The Profit*, he describes a mentor or teacher as one who "does not bid you enter the house of his wisdom, but rather leads you to the threshold of your own mind." Mike Murdock says in his book, The Wisdom Commentary, that, "there are two ways to receive wisdom: 1) mistakes; and 2) mentors. Mentors are the difference between poverty and prosperity; decrease and increase; loss and gain; pain and pleasure; deterioration and restoration" (pg. 141).

The protégé will:
- invest everything to stay in the presence of the mentor
- follow the counsel of the mentor
- reveal the secrets and dreams of his heart to the mentor
- freely discuss his mistakes and pain with the mentor
- clearly define his expectations to his mentor
- gladly sow seeds of appreciation back into the life of the mentor

- ultimately receive the mantle of the mentor he serves
- move toward the shelter of the mentor during a season of attack and warfare
- change his own schedule to invest time in the presence of the mentor
- discern, respect, and pursue the answers God has stored in the mentor for their life." (pg. 184-5)

3. Continue your education. According to the U.S. Census Bureau in 2012, high school dropouts will earn, over the course of their lifetime, roughly $250,000 less than high school graduates. They are also more likely to suffer ill health, get involved in drugs and crime, and die younger.

Learning is a lifelong process, and much of the good stuff to be learned is not taught in school. You will be the same person five years from now, except for the BOOKS you read, the VIDEOS you watch, the AUDIOS you listen to, and the PEOPLE you choose to associate with. Again, much of the most important things one needs to learn in life are not taught in school. You have to seek these valuable lessons elsewhere and on your own.

BOOKS. I am not a fast reader, but during the course of a formal education in which I earned a Bachelors, Masters, Doctoral degrees and post-Doctoral education at several universities, I have read a lot of fat, meaty, often dull text-books and other required reading. Of far greater influence in my life have been the multitude of skinny little paperbacks, about attitude, goal setting, relationships, overcoming, and other personal growth topics. I've read hundreds of novels and have accumulated a library of thousands of books. My books were my friends with whom I enjoyed spending time. I say were because in our recent move, we downsized, and I gave away 95% of those accumulated books.

Often, I would come home with an armload of newly purchased reading material, and Molly would fuss that I should go to the library instead of spending so much money on books. My reply would always be, "Listen, I don't smoke. I don't drink. I don't run around with wild women. Let me buy some books."

The three most impactful books I have ever read are: *The Greatest Story Ever Told* by Fulton Oursler, *This Was Your Life* by Rick Howard and Jamie Lash, and *Fathered by God* by John Eldredge. A couple of years ago, I loaned a copy of all three of these to a very fine younger man in whom I had a special interest in helping. I made the strong recommendation that he read these books which had so impacted my life. I guaranteed him that they would impact his too, if only he would peruse them. After a year of not even reading the first page of any, he gave the books back saying, "I'm just not a reader." As Mark Twain said,

> *Somebody who won't read, has no advantage over the person who can't read.*

What a tragedy. What a lost opportunity. What an example of unteachability. I was so disappointed. I had looked forward to spending time with him, discussing with him the ideas within those books, and finding out what was meaningful to him. Unfortunately, what could have been a special bonding experience between us never took place. Being unteachable is a terrible handicap in life. It is hard to improve when one is unteachable.

AUDIOS. When I was working as a school administrator in suburban Philadelphia years ago, I had an hour commute each way to work every day. During the winter, I would leave home in the dark, get to school as the sun was coming up, and arrive back home once again in the dark. Some people spend that kind of commuting time - day after day, week after week, month after month, and year after year - with nothing to show for all that down time, except perhaps an accident or a traffic ticket or two. What a perfect opportunity instead to invest that time by listening to motivating and/or instructional audios. You pick the topics. There are tons of materials available for you to learn about things that interest you, again, things that were not taught in school. It only makes sense to turn those otherwise unproductive hours of commuting into something constructive that will help you improve.

VIDEOS. Unlike audios, for obvious reasons, videos are not recommended while driving. However, once again, there is a limitless supply of instructional videos available on the Internet. You can learn about anything you want simply by going on your computer, or smart phone, typing in what information you seek, and selecting a suitable source. As Donny Miller said, "In the age of information, ignorance is a choice!"

PEOPLE. As a teenager, my mother used to tell me all the time, "You get like the company you keep." Those were real words of wisdom that I took to heart so that I ran around with nice, solid, well-adjusted, trouble-free friends in high school and college. Being a teenager is difficult enough without falling into the wrong crowd, since "groupthink" and "peer pressure" become so dominant during those years. Just so you know, the definition of a teenager is "someone who is too old to do what kids do. They are too young to do what grownups do. So, they do all the crazy things nobody else will do."

If one runs around with winners, you begin to think like a winner; it rubs off by association. In like manner, if one keeps company with losers, the inevitable occurs and you begin thinking like a loser. Whichever your choice, behavior follows thinking, action follows thought, and all too soon those actions bring trouble. Companions can be either lift you up or contribute to your downfall. Choose your friends wisely. On the flipside, if you are a loner, a hermit, or without a social circle, then the tendency is to play the same thoughts and biases repeatedly in your mind, without new input from which to grow.

They say that the ideal tennis partner is a slightly better player than you. Best not to have someone who is so much better that they totally dominate your game and make you feel inept. It is equally unsatisfying to play with a weaker opponent than you, as that is no fun either, wastes your time, makes you play sloppily, and teaches you nothing. I think it is similar in choosing friends. Choose those who challenge you to be better and bring value to a relationship of mutual benefit.

4. In your efforts to become your best you, don't forget the little stuff from day to day. "Little things mean a lot!" Check yourself against this suggested list of good practices from Robert Rohm in his Tip of the Week blog on *personalityinsights.com*.

1. Keep your word.
2. Keep your appointments and be on time (despite the occasional downside that no one may be there to appreciate your punctuality).
3. Pay your bills.
4. Don't talk badly about other people or talk behind their back.
5. Always be respectful of women and treat them as you would want another man to treat your mother.
6. Keep your hair dry and your feet warm, and you'll hardly ever be sick.

And I would add another: Manage your thoughts. James Allen in his wonderful little book entitled, As A Man Thinketh advances the idea that we, people, are "makers of themselves by virtue of the thoughts which they choose and encourage." Allen, expounding on Proverbs 23:7 (KJV), which says, "For as he thinketh in his heart, so is he…" goes on to say, "A man is literally what he thinks, his character being the complete sum of all his thoughts."

There is one personal quality, above all others to covet and cultivate and that is persistence! This is the never say die, never quit attitude that is the biggest difference maker between success and failure. Former British Prime Minister, Winston Churchill, during the dark days of 1941, gave one of his most famous and often misquoted speeches. He was speaking to the all-boys Harrows School, and he said, "Never give in—never, never, never, never, except to convictions of honour and good sense."

One of America's premier motivational speakers of his

time was Zig Ziglar. When asked him about retirement, he displayed the enthusiasm and can-do attitude for which he was known by answering, "I'm not going to ease up, back up, let up, slow up, or give up until I'm taken up!"

Finally, former President Calvin Coolidge gave this summarizing quote about persistence, "Nothing in this world can take the place of persistence. Talent will not: nothing is more common than unsuccessful men with talent. Genius will not; unrewarded genius is almost a proverb. Education will not; the world is full of educated derelicts. Persistence and determination alone are omnipotent!"

For years now, I have used the following worthy sequence in framing the consequence of one's choices. It seemed to be the proper thing with which to sum up this chapter about consciously and continually striving to improve yourself. I'll end with the following wisdom from Lao Tzu:

Watch your thoughts, they become your words.

Watch your words, they become your actions.

Watch your actions, they become your habits.

Watch your habits, they become your character.

Watch your character, it becomes your destiny!

CHAPTER FIVE

The MOST Important Choice

Choosing Your Lord

A Story. I am neither a theologian nor a dedicated Bible scholar. At age 92, I stand before you as a sinner saved by the grace of a forgiving Savior. The following is my story, and I know there is no more important decision to be made in life than the decision to follow Jesus. I learned as a child when I sang in Sunday school during the 1930s at the Calvary Presbyterian Church in Highland Park, Upper Darby, Pennsylvania:

"Jesus loves me, this I know, for the Bible tells me so

Little ones to Him belong, they are weak, but He is strong

Yes, Jesus loves me, yes, Jesus loves me

Yes, Jesus loves me; the Bible tells me so."

Several decades ago, at the Sunday morning worship service at a Yager business conference in Hampton Rhodes, Virginia, thousands stood mesmerized as my friend Tony Renard played that spiritually simple hymn in his inimitable piano style. Tony created an emotional, heartwarming moment causing many of us to tear up as memories of a happy, innocent childhood came flooding back.

I learned as a simple, trusting child that I was a child

of God; that in addition to a biological father who sired me, and a kind, gentle man who was the father who raised me, I also had a Heavenly Father to whom I could pray. This one is called the *Lord's Prayer*, and I recite it to start my nightly prayers:

> *Our Father who art in heaven, hallowed be thy name. Thy kingdom come. Thy will be done on earth as it is in heaven. Give us this day our daily bread and forgive us our trespasses as we forgive those who trespass against us. Lead us not into temptation but deliver us from evil for Thine is the kingdom, the power, and the glory forever and ever. Amen"*

I begin my prayer time with the Lord's Prayer because, while I hate to admit it, I have been known to fall asleep talking to my Lord and want to submit something in case and before that occurs. Now, how bad is that? To fall asleep while talking to the Almighty? I'm embarrassed to reveal that. My only rationalization could be that, perhaps, I'm not the only sinner who has done that. The spirit is willing, but the flesh is weak.

We need not overcomplicate things with our worldly sophistication, logic, or false pride. As Jesus taught in Matthew 18:3-4,

> *Verily I say to you, Except ye be converted, and become as little children, ye shall not enter into the kingdom of heaven. Whosoever therefore shall humble himself as this little child, the same is greatest in the kingdom of heaven.*

Back in that church in Highland Park is where my memory tells me my walk of faith began. I became aware at an early age that I had three fathers, unlike most little boys. As my story unfolds, you will see that I had a Heavenly Father, a biological father, and a father who adopted and raised me. How blessed was I?

During the 1920s, my biological mother emigrated to Philadelphia from Scotland. I never knew nor sought much information about her. I felt satisfied where I was and just wasn't curious. Her sisters, my aunts, did tell me some things about my birth mother. They said she was tall, intelligent, caring, and a decent person. She was trained as a nurse and began working for a medical doctor who, in August of 1929, impregnated her with me without the benefit of marriage. In our American culture of that time, this was a huge moral mistake frowned upon by society. So too was abortion as a solution to that problem of illegitimacy. Rather than be born as a bastard child, I would have become an abortion statistic by today's standards and not had a life. I have a stand to take in the abortion controversy. It is part of my story.

A Related Warning

In his two revealing books, *The Harbinger* and *The Harbinger II*, Jonathan Cahn tells of how parents sacrificed their children by the thousands to the god Bael in ancient Israel. He says that God withdrew His protection from His chosen people due to those evil practices. The country of ancient Israel, as a result, suffered for many years for their disobedience. Everyone should know that there are consequences for disobedience to God! The main point in both of Jonathan Cahn's books is to warn us, as a nation, that we cannot continue in disobedience either, without risking the loss of God's protection.

Our republic was founded by Godly men who dedicated our country to Him! Remember the wisdom of comedian Jeff Foxworthy, who said, "Our country was founded by geniuses, and today is being run by idiots!"

From our Godly inception and dedication to Him, the USA has thus prospered like no other nation in history. Yet, increasingly in recent years, our leadership has taken God out of our schools. Our current lawmakers ignore Him in their proposed and implemented policies. We continue to abort fetuses of unwanted children under the guise of a mother's right to choose. This barbaric practice has resulted in the deaths of well beyond those thousands of children sacrificed in ancient Israel. The numbers have exploded into the tens of millions here in America alone. Many abortions today are even cruel late-term abortions, where the babies about to be born can feel pain. They have a complete nervous system, heartbeat, and an active brain. Yet it is my understanding that they are cut apart, dismembered, and suffer a horrible death!

Reverend Cahn warns that, as a country, we need to change our ways, or we may suffer the same fate as ancient Israel. Today, many of us are concerned God will withdraw His protection from our republic. When we examine the current state of our country, we might even wonder: Has our protection already been withdrawn? Well, we know God is in charge!

> If my people, who are called by my name, will
> humble themselves, and pray, and seek my face,
> and turn from their wicked ways, then I will hear
> from heaven, and I will forgive their sin, and will
> heal their land. (2 Chronicles 7:14)

Back to the Story

My birth mother left me in an orphanage. Then, her sister and her husband, who became my Aunt Mattie and Uncle Bill, came to the rescue. My birth mother went off in disgrace to Windsor, Ontario, Canada, to live out her life. (She died at age 96, a clue as to my good genes.) Aunt Mattie had just had a child of her own, Gladys, and felt unable to take on another infant at the time. After the crash of '29, the economic depression of the 1930s was in full rampage. My Uncle Bill was a butcher at a small grocery store near where my soon-to-be adoptive parents lived. My soon-to-be adoptive mother and Uncle Bill, being the two gregarious people they were, neither of whom ever met a stranger, struck up a friendship. From conversations, Uncle Bill learned that my parents were childless and looking to adopt. So, I was indeed at the right place at the right time, and the adoption deal was struck. Uncle Bill and Aunt Mattie became my favorite aunt and uncle, and Bill's outgoing customer, along with her husband, became my parents.

Bill and Mattie moved to the Washington D.C. area, but our two families visited each other frequently during my youth so that Gladys and I got be friends as well as cousins. After many decades of lost contact, Gladys and I were recently reconnected through the website of a popular DNA database.

My new parents told me about my adoption from an early age, so I never had any hang-ups about it. Actually, my parents told me that I was CHOSEN, which made me feel special. This information was a good thing. One of my high school friends found out by accident in the tenth grade that he was adopted. It was like a ton of bricks had fallen on him. He really got upset, felt he had been deceived, and became very resentful and bitter about it.

During my youth, my parents saw that I regularly got to church, Sunday School, Vacation Bible School, and Boy Scouts. They set an excellent example for many years. My father served as a faithful elder in the Presbyterian church we attended. At the same time, my mother put on numerous covered dish suppers at church. Both parents were respected, active participants and contributors in our church commu- nity. As a result, my childhood and teen social life revolved around the church, the Boy Scout Troop, and the families and friends there.

Then, along came my backsliding, rebellious years that began toward the end of high school and continued through college, my time in the army, and into the mid- '70s. It was not that I became anti-religious or disavowed the beliefs I had been taught; rather, I just ignored them. I didn't attend church, I didn't pray or read the Bible, and I didn't act as a Christian should. I was sinful, selfish, and stupid, all caught up in the stresses of my own life, advancement, and career. During that time, I felt that I was unworthy to be called a Christian.

Then during the '70s, because of my fortunate associa- tion with Godly leaders in the Amway business, I began to seek the Lord prayerfully. I asked Him to rid me of my sin- ful, selfish, stupid ways and help me get better every day. From the evangelist and author Mike Murdock, I learned that "God never responds to tears and pain, but He always responds to pursuit." The Lord answered my prayers so that my spiritual, personal, and financial life all began to turn around and improve. His faithfulness brought me back in step once again with the Lord.

I now pray daily for my family, lest any of them fall away from their Christian spiritual roots and politically conservative upbringing, as I did before them. As I approach the latter years of my life, the words from Psalm 71:18 come to mind, with a clear commitment I feel pressing in urgency upon me.

> *Even when I am old and gray, do not forsake me,*
> *my God, till I declare your power to the next gen-*
> *eration.*

During that infamous "mid-life crisis" period of their life, many others don't even want to discuss spiritual or political matters. They erroneously conclude that they are enlightened but seem blinded and not open to seeking the truth. I take courage that perhaps, those too will come back and lead their family spiritually because of Proverbs 22:6, which states, "Train up a child in the way he should go: and when he is old, he will not depart from it." So that is one moral of my story.

Another moral of my story is that I feel I have been hugely blessed in life despite my sinful meandering. The Lord has granted me extra time and kept me alive for some assignment of His, to hopefully correct and make up for my earlier wandering. For example, I feel incredibly blessed because I have undergone three near-death experiences during my life.

The first occurred when I was three years old. I contracted pneumonia, was very sick for a long time, and almost died. But I lived and was, as a result, a skinny, scrawny kid up through my teens. I became not only the tallest kid in my class, but I was also the youngest, having turned seventeen shortly before graduation from high school. I was a late bloomer.

The second time took place in the early 1990s. My wife and I were going to a significant business function in San Jose, California. On the way out there, we stopped in Nashville for the night. We had a covered dish supper and met with a group of our business team. The following day, I awoke feeling terrible with a very queasy stomach. I thought it must have been something I had eaten the previous night at the covered dish. We debated not going on, to instead return home, but I decided to tough it out. We had responsibilities at the function and didn't want to let anyone down. The plane ride was long and uncomfortable. I ignored the meal service as just the smell of food brought back that queasy sensation.

On arrival in San Jose, I felt weak and unable to carry all our bags. Fortunately, Bob Bolin, a friend, fellow business leader, and former Major League Baseball pitcher, in an act of spontaneous kindness, helped me in handling my bags into the hotel. After resting briefly, Molly and I attended an afternoon meeting of the senior leadership. I did not feel like eating anything all day. That Thursday, I sent Molly to the evening meeting and returned to our room to curl up in bed for the night.

A growing pain developed in my abdomen as I lay there. Then at about 1:30 Friday morning, my whole body began shaking convulsively and violently. The pain was intense. I felt terrible, didn't know what was happening to me, and had never experienced anything like it. Molly had not yet come back from the meeting, so I suffered alone. There are just some things you have to do by yourself. Nobody can do it for you. Suffering is one of those things. Then, as suddenly as it started, it stopped. The shaking stopped. The pain stopped. I felt relief and calmly fell asleep.

Friday morning, when I awoke, I felt a little better for a change. I thought that whatever it was, I had survived to live another day. As things turned out, that became "barely survived." Over, it was not! They say that the five most dangerous words in medicine are, "Maybe it will go away." My appetite had not returned, so I only ate a little breakfast. We relaxed some and then went to the Friday afternoon leadership meeting.

I was having trouble concentrating during the meeting and was starting to feel worse. By late afternoon, my good Christian friend Merritt Wiese, who was sitting next to me, leaned over and said to me, "Do you feel alright? You look terrible. You look almost green." I told him a little of what had happened. He suggested I ought to lie down. I took his advice, went back to our room, and did.

The problem was that Molly and I were listed among the hosts for the general session that evening. When we arrived at the hosts' meeting, I discovered that our duties were spread out throughout the evening, from early to late. I pulled aside Doyle Yager, who was in charge. By the way, Doyle is not only brilliant, but he handles details well. He has a servant's heart, a ministerial manner, is attentive, and is a most compassionate and understanding fellow. My impression of Doyle was reinforced that night. I told him I was having some challenges and asked could he re-arrange things so my duties would be concentrated early in the evening. I wasn't sure I could make it through the whole program. He went to the trouble and obligingly changed things around, which I greatly appreciated. I left the evening function as early as I could. Then, Saturday morning, I woke up with these words for Molly, "Enough of this. I'm not getting any better. Get me to the hospital!"

We taxied over to the San Jose Hospital, which I later learned was in a bad part of town. The emergency room proved to be a big and busy place, with much hustle, noise, and many people coming and going. I was put in a bed within a cubicle with curtains drawn to give some privacy. The day dragged on through a series of tests and multiple distractions.

I had fallen asleep but was awakened by loud screaming and frantic activity in the next cubicle. I found out later that a young woman who was the victim of an automobile accident had her leg sheared off just below the knee. Her case and some other emergencies took priority over me. So, I just lay there listening to all this trauma around me.

I remember thinking, I don't know what kind of problem I've got, but there are people here with worse problems. Isn't that a good way to put your situation in perspective? Start feeling sorry for yourself, and then weigh your problems against the struggles of others you may know. There probably aren't very many people with whom you'd be willing to swap lives given the opportunity. All of us can choose our attitude. I used to think and say that attitude was everything. Then I heard internationally esteemed expert on leadership John Maxwell say, "Attitude is not everything. It cannot make up for talent nor intelligence, but it is THE difference maker." When overwhelmed with problems and tempted to embrace victim mentality, sing this old hymn I love from Vacation Bible School decades ago. Count Your Blessings.

> *Count your blessings, name them one by one.*
> *Count your blessings, see what God has done.*
> *Count your blessings, name them one by one.*
> *Count your many blessings, see what God has*
> *done.*

After being ignored most of the day, finally, at about 7 pm, a doctor came in and said, "Sorry for keeping you waiting, but we can't wait any longer. You've had a ruptured appendix since it popped very early Friday morning. Infection has spread through your body, and you have about an hour to live unless we do something, which we are going to do right now." That is the last thing I remember until I awoke in a daze sometime Sunday afternoon to see Molly at my bedside.

Dexter and Dennis Delisle came to see me in the hospital on Sunday afternoon after the function and after my operation. Their visit was much appreciated. I'll not forget their kindness.

I remained in bed for five days with a tube inserted into my abdomen to drain off infectious fluids. I was doped up and in a stupor for a few days, but I remember my annoyance at being awakened too frequently for checks, pills, and probing. Molly dutifully and faithfully stuck with me throughout the week, which was inconvenient for her. Finally, I was released from the hospital to fly back home on Friday. I was as limp as a wet dishrag, had no energy, and did nothing, and I mean NOTHING, for three weeks. It took that long to recover and get back my strength.

My third near-death experience occurred in the first year of the 21st Century. We had recently bought a beautiful lakeside property with almost 1000 feet of shoreline on Lake Murray in South Carolina. We lived in the original cottage while we began building our dream home of about 8,000 square feet. When taking vitamins, I had always taken them one pill at a time. Then I saw my mentor Dexter take his by the handful and gulp them down with water. So, one day in our cottage, I decided to up the quantity to be more efficient. I popped three large C vitamins into my mouth, added a swallow of water, and guess what happened? Two went down just fine, and one got stuck. I couldn't breathe in, and I couldn't exhale either. I knew I was in BIG trouble. Fortunately, Molly was nearby, heard me struggling, and rushed to the rescue. First, she tried to do the Heimlich maneuver on me, but I was too big and tall. By this time, my face was red, and I only had a few seconds left before I passed out (probably instead, I would have passed on). Molly pushed me into the bathroom, bent me over the sink, wound up, and whacked me as hard as she could on the back. That pill came out of my mouth like it was shot from a gun, and I gulped in a lifesaving breath of air. She literally saved my life!

I tell you these three examples from my own experience to illustrate that life is precious, fragile, and can unexpectedly be snatched away from us. No one knows the time and place of when our death may occur. I would guess that any of you can name people you may have known that died prematurely and unexpectedly. So anticipate, and as the Boy Scout motto states, BE PREPARED!

Reasons

Your most important choice in life is to choose Jesus because you literally will be lost without Him and His teachings, just as sure as you would be trying to navigate the Alaskan wilderness without a compass. Time in history is measured by His birth, BC or AD. How significant is that? Does that not give massive credence to His life, His sacrifice for us, what He stands for, and what He teaches.

His coming as our Messiah was predicted hundreds of years in advance by the prophet Isaiah.

> *For to us a child is born, to us a Son is given: and*
> *the government shall*
> *be upon His shoulder: and His name shall be called*
> *Wonderful, Counselor,*
> *The Mighty God, The Everlasting Father, The*
> *Prince of Peace. (Isaiah 9:6)*

An angel announced his birth to shepherds abiding in the field, keeping watch over their flocks by night.

> *And, lo, the angel of the Lord came upon them,*
> *and the glory of the Lord*
> *shone round about them: and they were sore*
> *afraid. And the angel said to*
> *them, Fear not, for, behold, I bring you good tid-*
> *ings of great joy, which*
> *shall be to all people. (Luke 2:9)*

Jesus' words have served as spiritual direction for the entirety of western civilization. So, what's your problem with buying into His story? Maybe your trouble in believing and having childlike faith in Holy Scripture has its roots in hearing the story of Jonah and the whale.

Now the Lord prepared a great fish to swallow up
Jonah. And Jonah was in the belly of the fish three
days and three nights. (Jonah 2:17)

Then from Jonah 2:10,

And the Lord spoke to the fish, and it vomited out
Jonah upon the dry land.

Now admittedly, if you will pardon the pun, that is a tall fish tale to swallow. However, with the Lord God almighty, all things are possible.

I will personalize a joke I heard about this well-known Bible story. My childhood friend Jackie and I were walking back home from Sunday school after our teacher, Mrs. Ide, had just finished teaching us the lesson of Jonah and the whale.

Jackie repeatedly said, "I just can't believe that anybody could spend three days in the sea, in the belly of a fish. I don't think that is possible."

So finally, I said to Jackie, "Well, when I get to heaven, I'm going to see Jonah and ask him all about that."

Jackie then asked, "What if he's not there?"

I replied, "Then you ask him!"

Each of us in this country has been given freedom to choose many things in life. We can choose what to do, where to go, how much to spend, where to live, who to vote for, what friends we have, and what we believe. Choosing your Lord, who you will follow, who you will obey, is THE most crucial decision in your lifetime!

Is the Bible truly the inerrant, inspired word of God or not? Was Jesus the Son of God, a real person, sent to live among us and die a horrible death to save us from ourselves? His life is the greatest story ever told or the greatest hoax ever perpetrated on humankind. It is your choice to believe or not.

As I said in Chapter Two, choosing a mate is so important because it significantly affects one's whole life. I warned that it is best if you make the right choice the first time. But if you don't, you can still adjust and overcome that bad decision — but not without pain. The choice before you in choosing your Lord is far more important than choosing a mate for life. In choosing a mate, you can change course, correct that mistake, and begin again. However, upon death, whether you chose Jesus or not, you are stuck with your choice for all eternity!

Choosing your Lord is actually part of choosing to fix yourself, as addressed in the previous chapter. Suppose you choose to better yourself according to this world's standards—you get healthier, advance your education or career, or increase your wealth. In that case, you have improved your life for a relatively short period of time. Choosing the Lord improves your life for eternity. And your mate can be with you for eternity if you both get this choice right. Think! You better get it right, for the consequences of your decision will impact your life on this Earth. The blessings you and your family may or may not receive will carry on through eternity. Samuel Shoemaker said, "Eternal life does not begin with death; it begins with faith."

Knowledge can come from FACTS or FAITH. As to faith, it comes through clearly in this hymn so beautifully written by E. Margaret Clarkson:

THIS I KNOW

I do not know what next may come

Across my pilgrim way,
I do not know tomorrow's road,
Nor see beyond today,
But this I know—My Savior knows
The path I cannot see,
And I can trust His wounded hand
To guide and care for me.
I do not know what may befall
Of sunshine or of rain,
I do not know what may be mine
Of pleasure and of pain,
But this I know—my Savior knows
And whatsoe'er it be,
Still, I can trust His love to give
What will be best for me.
I do not know what may await
Or what the morrow brings,
But with the glad salute of faith
I hail its opening wings!
For this I know—that in my Lord
Shall all my needs be met,
And I can trust the heart of Him
Who has not failed me yet.

Jeremiah Johnston wrote,

Faith and the mind are not at odds; faith is not
believing in nonsense, faith is not embracing
unreasonable, illogical things. In short, faith is
not stupid... Faith is intelligent; it is educated; it is
learned; it is hungry for understanding. A healthy
faith is a seeking faith. A healthy faith is not satis-
fied to be ignorant, to be naïve, to remain in the
dark, or to pass on misinformation.

You don't want to chance getting this choice wrong.
You have everything to gain and such an enormity to lose.

Proverbs 3:5-6 says

> *Trust in the Lord with all your heart, and lean not*
> *to your own understanding. In all ways acknowl-*
> *edge Him, and He will direct your paths.*

This scripture tells us we will not be lost if we trust and follow Him. Another scripture suggests that you choose, then submit to Him. "A man plans his way, but the Lord directs his steps" Proverbs 16:9. What a dynamic duo when we team with the Lord.

How great is your own understanding? How great is your arrogance that you would reject His direction and seek your own way? You are doomed and will miss out on blessings and personal satisfaction that otherwise would come to you.

> *And we know that in all things God works for the*
> *good of those who love Him, who have been called*
> *to His purpose. Romans 8:28*

Tom Landry, legendary Dallas Cowboys coach, said, "I found success as a football coach. I found fulfillment in my salvation by way of Jesus Christ." Simply follow Him by asking Him into your heart, by asking Him to show you the way, and by submitting to His direction.

The saying goes, "Everybody wants to go to heaven, but nobody wants to die." The fact is that everybody is going to die, but not everyone is going to heaven. Some, by not choosing Jesus will, by abdication, choose eternal damnation, suffering, and pain... forever! The only path to heaven is by a profession of faith in Jesus Christ!

Christians are accused of being judgmental and rigid in their thinking. I suppose it could be said. However, on some things, there simply can be no compromise.

For God so loved the world, that He gave His only
begotten Son, that whosoever believes in Him
should not perish, but have everlasting life. (John
3:16)

Atheists are equally adamant. The difference is that their conclusion, not to believe, is manufactured. Our conclusion comes from God. God either is or isn't. The Bible is either the accumulated word of God or not. Either or! For example, The Ten Commandments are not The Ten Suggestions. God saw that the people needed moral direction but were not strong enough to abide by The Ten Commandments alone, so he sent His son to live among us, teach us new ways, and take on our sins in sacrifice. When it comes to God and Jesus, you either buy the whole package, or you do not. You cannot cherry-pick parts you like and reject parts that you don't. It is your choice, all or nothing!

OK, so you understand that you will someday die, but none of us know when. Think about it. Even though we know death is coming eventually, many of us are caught by surprise with death coming prematurely, totally unprepared for our end-of-life event. Recently, terrible tornadoes swept through Kentucky for an unprecedented 200 miles, surprising over 100 people with premature death. Are you willing to gamble on your end time and chance being caught unprepared to face the eternal consequences of your nondecision?

In his "Choose This Day" devotional, David Jeremiah's message fits perfectly with the focus of this chapter. First, he cites Deuteronomy 30:19, which says, "I call heaven and earth as witnesses today against you, that I have set before you life and death, blessing and cursing; therefore choose life, that both you and your descendants may live." He continues,

> *Every parent has been through the 'it's your*
> *choice' exercise with their children. They set out*
> *two alternatives, two possibilities, two choices—as*
> *well as the ramifications of each choice—and then*
> *let the child choose and live with the following*
> *consequences. Sometimes, life gives us choices,*
> *the consequences of which are unknown. So, we*
> *have to make our best decision and move forward.*
> *But in the spiritual and moral realms, choices are*
> *much clearer.*

Jeremiah further explains, "When Moses was preparing the Israelites to inhabit the Promised Land of Canaan, he set before them two ways of life: "life and good" or "death and evil" (Deuteronomy 30:15). He had previously spelled out the consequences of each way of life for them. Walking in covenant with God would bring life and blessing, but rejecting God's ways would bring death and destruction. Joshua reiterated these choices to them again years later. 'Choose for yourselves this day whom you will serve' Joshua 24:15."

We are to be in this world but not of this world. We must choose. We cannot adhere to the world's standards and serve Jesus.

> *No man can serve two masters: for either he will*
> *hate the one, and love the other; or else he hold to*
> *the one and despise the other. Ye cannot serve God*
> *and mammon. (Matthew 6:24)*

What we believe is not necessarily the truth. For many, it is what our current culture tells us is true. Too many fall prey to whatever the media spins. Too often, these are lies presented as the truth to those gullible enough to be suckered in by it. Too many people want something to be true because it confirms what they want to believe. Why do some people harden their hearts with irrational hostility, making them aggressive towards something they haven't thoroughly investigated?

Everyone has heard of a health malady that befalls some of the elderly called "hardening of the arteries." Worse to take upon oneself is a "hardening of the attitudes." Some people are born stubborn. Others adopt that attitude going through life, concluding that they are right. Most everybody thinks they are right and have the truth when they all do not! Jeremiah Johnston said, "One of the most dangerous places to be is when we don't seek truth." The major world religions — including Christianity, Islam, Hinduism, Buddhism, and Judaism—all believe they have the truth. Be open to pursuing the truth as there is so much PR, spin, misinformation, untruths, and blatant lies circulating about spiritual matters. Consider the source of information in judging its validity.

Here is a question for those of you who either do not believe in, or choose not to follow, or be obedient to Jesus. How can you expect to receive God's blessings while on Earth if you ignore Him, fail to pursue Him, and are not obedient to His ways? Do you ever feel frustrated? Do you feel like you are on a hamster wheel going round and round, struggling to advance but going nowhere? Well then, connect the dots! If you live a life separate from Him, what can you expect? Frankly, what more do you deserve? Get with the program before it is too late! Don't procrastinate. My mother used to tell me, "Procrastination is the thief of time." You will have choices to make as the clock ticks, the days go by, and your life continues. So, choose life and blessings by selecting to follow the ways of the Lord.

Perhaps you are doing great sailing your ship on your own. You are master of your fate. You are happy and leading an extraordinary life by worldly standards. You are successful, competent, ethical, and accepted by those around you. Yet you reject the Bible specifically and Christianity as a whole. Most who do so have never read the Bible or learned about the life of Christ. To reject something so important without the due process of investigation is to be super arrogant or blatantly stupid. Are you offended by such an accusation? You don't think of yourself as arrogant or stupid. OK then, if you won't read the Bible, I dare you to read *The Greatest Story Ever Told* by Fulton Oursler, one of the three most impactful books of my life I mentioned earlier. Don't be arrogant. Neither be you ignorant.

Consequences

Immediately upon death, non-believers are judged and cast into hell (a real place of eternal damnation, discomfort, suffering, and pain). It doesn't matter whether you were a nice guy in life. It doesn't matter if you were generous, that you were considerate of others, or that you never cheated someone in a business deal, or that you were kind to animals. These are not the criteria for determining whether you will spend eternity in heaven or hell. WHERE YOU SPEND IT IS SOLELY BASED UPON YOUR PROFESSION OF FAITH IN, YOUR PURSUIT OF, AND YOUR OBEDIENCE TO JESUS CHRIST! That alone is your ticket to heaven. It is that simple. Absolutes, yes! Either or, yes! Black or white, yes! Your choice, yes again!

The path to eternal glory is a process. SALVATION is

the spiritual rescue from sin and death. JUSTIFICATION is that process by which we are saved from the penalty of our sins, the moment we receive Jesus. SANCTIFICATION is the ongoing process of becoming more like Jesus as we are set aside for His service. Finally, GLORIFICATION will occur when we are raptured or resurrected. Then, our bodies will be transformed for eternity.

In his TV sermon of January 30, 2022, David Jeremiah listed seven things we will encounter as we enter heaven:

1. A rousing welcome
2. A rich reward
3. A resurrected transformed body
4. A renewed assignment
5. The royal throne
6. A rapturous reunion
7. Being face to face with our risen Savior

If you want to find out more about what you can anticipate in heaven, I encourage you to read *This Was Your Life*, by Rick Howard and Jamie Lash, or Bruce Wilkinson's book, *A Life God Rewards*. If you dare, examine the book by John Hagee, *The Three Heavens*. If you dare, check out the book *Heaven* by Randy Alcorn. Read David Jeremiah's book, *Revealing the Mysteries of Heaven*, if you dare. Only then, if you still can, tell me you are unwilling to take steps to ensure you will spend eternity there.

Become open to the idea, because whether you have thought so or not, up to this time, the decision to choose Jesus IS the most crucial choice you can ever make in life! That is why I have made this chapter the cornerstone and major concept of this book. If choosing your mate was the guts of this book, and choosing to better yourself was the brains of this book, then this chapter on choosing Jesus is the heart of this book!

I would like to close this most important chapter about your most important choice with the words of two good old hymns that have been written to open the door and reach out to you.

Open my eyes that I may see
glimpses of truth thou hast for me.
Place in my hands the wonderful key
that shall unclasp and set me free.
Silently now I wait for thee,
ready my God, thy will to see.
Open my eyes, illumine me,
Spirit divine!

As well as this one:

Softly and tenderly, Jesus is calling,
Calling for you and for me.
See, on the portals He's waiting and watching,
watching for you and for me.
Come home, come home,
you who are weary come home;
earnestly, tenderly, Jesus is calling,
calling, O sinner, come home!

CHAPTER SIX

Afterthoughts and Other Choices

I have chosen to focus, thus far, on what I believe to be the three most important choices one can make in life. Our whole life consists of making one choice after another, never ceasing until we are dead. To keep any discussion of life in perspective, it is well to keep in mind that there are far more dead people than living, and their numbers are increasing. Life is that period that begins with birth and extends until death. It is a time we fill with something based on the choices we make. As John Lennon sang, "Life is what happens to you while you're busy making other plans." Life can be a worrisome time, but it can also bring opportunities. Gertrude Ellgas writes:

When doubts and fears are growing,
It's hard to keep on going
From day to day not knowing
Just what the end will be.
Take each day as you find it,
If things go wrong don't mind it
For each day leaves behind it
A chance to start anew.

In this chapter, I would like to characterize some other choices of significance that most of us face during our lifetime. These will be mentioned but not treated in the same detail as the first three for two reasons. First, I don't want them to detract from the BIG THREE just covered. You see, the first three totally dominate these OTHER CHOICES that follow. So, you better get those choices right in the first place! The following are spin-offs of the first three. Secondly, I didn't want this book to get too long. Now, let's look at some other important decisions most of you will face in your journey through life. These are not in any particular order.

Choosing Your Career

Many of us derive a massive piece of our identity from our career. I had the privilege of hearing football legend Lou Holtz speak, and he told us that our self-image should not come from the job we do but rather from how well we do our job. In other words, how well we do our work is as important, if not more important, than what we do for work. Take the story of the newly arrived preacher that Saint Peter was escorting around the streets of heaven as part of his orientation. The tour's culmination concluded with him being shown his residence for eternity. It was a modest log cabin. As they turned in the walkway to his house, the preacher looked down the street and noticed one of the angels showing a big, beautiful mansion to a taxi driver he knew from his hometown.

Somewhat perturbed, the preacher said to Saint Peter, "I don't mean to appear ungrateful, but I have faithfully preached the Word of God for 50 years, and I get this little log cabin while that taxi driver gets a big mansion? Why?"

Saint Peter replied softly, "Well, it appears that while you preached, people slept. When he drove, people prayed."

Once committed to a career choice, it becomes a life-long dedication for many. However, the end of World War II brought about a certain wanderlust, a curiosity, a less regional outlook, and a greater interest in and possibility of travel. In addition, more widespread and flexible job opportunities became available on a national and international scale, thus a chance to see more of the world. This has contributed to more population mobility and more flexible job choices.

People have come to change jobs and careers frequently, to a much greater degree than in times past. They often finish one career and begin a second, which may bear no relationship to the first. Take this example: a Walmart greeter excelled at his job, but he struggled to get to work on time. Again and again, his supervisor called him on the carpet about being late to work.

Finally, in desperation, the supervisor told the greeter what a fine representative the man was for the store. Still, his punctuality would have to improve or else. The supervisor observed, "I understand that you spent your career in the service. It seems to me that you should have learned there to be punctual. What did they say to you in the service when you arrived late to work?"

The greeter replied, "They saluted and said, 'Good morning, Admiral. Would you like your coffee now, sir?'"

As a high school guidance counselor, Director of Guidance, school administrator, and a university professor, I found that many young people have little idea of what is in store for them once they find themselves in the real world. So, my simple advice boils down to this: first, find a job and career that you like doing, where you feel comfortable, which teaches you something, and leads on to something better. Second, find something you have a talent for, do well, and do with ease; otherwise, you become a square peg in a round hole. A vocational misfit usually doesn't last long or work out well. As Andrew Carnegie said,

> A man will always be more effective when en-
> gaged in the sort of work he likes best. That is why
> one's major purpose in life should be of his own
> choice. People who drift through life performing
> work they do not like, merely because they must
> have an income as a means of living, seldom get
> more than a living from their labor.

I know a fine young man who, upon graduation from college, just took a job to have a job. It was a dead-end job that didn't lead to anything. He wasn't looking for a career; he was just looking for a paycheck. That isn't all bad, at first and up to a point, but the goal is to advance and learn something from the job. On the other hand, another fine young man I know gained some knowledge, and some mental maturity as well, by serving in the Army before college. He saw some of the world and was trained as a combat medic. He has become a serious, disciplined student doing exceedingly well in college and has focused on a medical career. He knows what he wants and is in pursuit of that goal.

For someone unhappy at school or at work, Monday morning is the worst time of the week. This is especially true in the winter. It is still dark. You are snug as a bug in a rug in your warm bed. You have to get up and put your bare feet on the cold floor. The heat has been turned down during the night, and even the temperature inside is biting. Getting out of bed is a difficult act of disciplined will. Have you been in that situation? Ah, of course, you have.

Let me tell you about a family whose teenage son was not a particularly gifted student and who ran with a somewhat questionable crowd. Everyday his parents had a tough time getting him out of bed, up, and off to school. They were telling their neighbor about it and explained that the solution had been simple. As it turns out, getting him out of bed for school was much easier after the kid got the nose ring he wanted!

And then there is the story of John. John didn't want to go to school in the first place and overslept. Finally, his mother came in and shook him awake. He complained to her that he didn't want to go to school. He whined, "The kids don't like me. The teachers talk about me in the faculty lounge. I'm behind in my work." His mother replied, "John, you have to face it and go; after all, you're the principal!"

Mike Huckabee wrote,

> *More important than what we are paid for our work is what we will become as a result of our work. Our character will become more important than the careers we follow.*

The bottom line is to find something you like to do and which you do well. Then, choose a career based on using your God-given talents to serve people.

Choosing Your Friends and Associates

My mother always shared what I came to think of as "motherisms." One was "Count your life by smiles. Count your age, not by years, but by friends." She emphasized choosing my friends wisely. She repeatedly said to me, "You are known by the company you keep." We passed on that same wisdom to our children. They followed that advice and thus escaped the trap of running with the wrong crowd into which so many teens fall. Because they are especially susceptible to group-think, teens become like those they hang out with. Those they run with form a considerable influence upon their life! Anyone who chooses to hang out with winners will begin thinking like a winner, which generally leads to becoming one. The reverse is also true. In life, there are winners and losers. It is a choice; decide!

Choosing to Make Wise Financial Decisions

This is an area where mentorship is particularly essential. One doesn't learn financial success by taking courses in finance from broke professors who teach economic theory. As Mike Murdock has said, it is discovered in either of two ways: mistakes or mentors! If a personal financial mentor is not available, take advantage of the wealth of public knowledge not taught in school. You must seek it on your own!

In his landmark book, *Rich Dad, Poor Dad*, Robert Kiyosaki shows how two competent fathers' thoughts led to radically different financial results. His first book led to his second best seller, *Cash Flow Quadrant*, which clearly explains the impact of various sources of income.

The many helpful books, audios, and videos by Dave Ramsey are also valuable sources of financial wisdom and common sense. When such useful sources of knowledge are so easily accessible, to not avail yourself of them is just dumb! Why wander in ignorance, bumbling along on your own, trial and error, hit-or-miss fashion?

Here are a few simple tidbits to consider in making wise financial choices:

1. **Live below your means.** It has been said often that a miser grows rich by seeming poor. An extravagant person grows poor by seeming rich. Kurt Kulpa, CPA, president of his successful accounting firm in Ft. Worth, Texas, has this saying on a plaque on his wall. "If your OUTGO is more than your INCOME, your UPKEEP will be your DOWNFALL." If you can't manage your money, getting more of it will not necessarily solve your problem unless you change your thinking!

2. **Don't borrow to buy and finance depreciating items, particularly over a long time.** Instead, save until you have the cash to buy. For example, to finance a car over five or seven years, when early on most of the money is going toward paying interest rather than reducing the principle, puts one behind the financial 8 ball, as you have more money invested than the car is worth.

3. **Pay off your home mortgage by paying more than is required.** During the early part of a loan, most of your payment goes to pay interest, not reduce the principle. Anything you pay beyond the required payment reduces the principle. Consider whether your mortgage rate is significantly below the percentage rate you can get with the same money put into investments. If the mortgage rate is 2 or 3% and investing the same money in an asset that brings a 10 to15% return, do the math.

4. **Understand delayed gratification.** Work first. Play second. The rich invest their money and spend what is left. The poor spend their money and invest whatever may be left, if any.

5. **Don't make any significant purchases unless both you and your spouse agree.** Also, don't selfishly spend. As the man of the house, don't serve yourself by spending your family resources on fishing or hunting equipment, trips by yourself or with your buddies, more tools and gadgets, etc. Instead, share by putting your limited resources into things that benefit both of you. Spend your vacations together as husband and wife.

6. **Understand that the borrower is always at the mercy of the lender, so get out of debt.** ASAP. Today, slaves are no longer in chains; they are in debt! As the joke says, creditors have better, more accurate memories than their debtors!

7. **Don't lend any money to a friend or relative.** There is a good chance that it won't end up being a loan. Likely you will lose both your money and your friend. This has happened to us. Our friend took advantage of our good will but then felt guilty. He didn't want to look us in the eye, so he disappeared. In the case of a relative, who will always be part of your circle, chances are they will be back with another plea for you to help them out, just this one more time. They will become dependent on your benevolence if you allow it.

8. **In terms of what the future might bring, expect the best, but prepare for the worst.**

9. **Only take advice from those who stand to benefit from your success.** That is the only true win-win situation.

10. **Pay your bills on time.** Some people pay their bills when due. Some pay when overdue. Some never do. Bits and Pieces tells a story about an angry worker who goes to his payroll office to complain that his paycheck was $50 short. The payroll supervisor checks the books and says, "I see here

that on the last payday you were overpaid by $50. I don't recall you complaining about that." The worker huffed up a little and said, "Well I don't mind an occasional error, but this makes two in a row!"

11. **Develop multiple streams of income.** If you only have one, you are not in charge, they are. You are at the mercy of your employer and thus dependent upon them. As the adage says, "Don't put all your eggs in one basket." A study reported in 2017 concluded that 25% of Social Security recipients depend on it for at least 90% of their household income. BIG MISTAKE! In 2022, the average Social Security benefit payment was around $1,600 a month, or less than $20,000 a year. Also, it does not appear to be a dependable source, long term.

12. **As a matter of principle, don't depend on the government, period!**

13. **Confucius say: "When prosperity comes, do not use all of it!"**

14. **Stash a liquid emergency fund and don't touch it except for a real emergency.** Financial expert Dave Ramsey recommends starting with $1,000 in emergency funds. After you become debt free, you should save up enough to cover three- to six-months' worth of living expenses. According to a 2019 survey by the U.S. Federal Reserve, the mean bank account balance — for savings and checking accounts combined—was $5,300.

15. **You won't have a "wad" if you are not a "tightwad."**

16. **Being broke is a temporary condition.** Poverty is a state of mind.

17. **The higher one gets on the ladder of financial suc-**

cess, the more comfortable the rungs become. I might also add that the higher you are on the ladder of success, your rear end is more exposed to being shot at by those below.

18. **You not only have to be able to afford a significant purchase, but you also must be able to insure, maintain, and repair it.** Many people fail to factor in the cost of upkeep after the initial purchase. Upkeep is a considerable drain on expenses in a depreciating item like a car, boat, or motor home. When it comes to accumulating material things and living an enhanced lifestyle, remember Mathew 6:33, "But seek you first the kingdom of God and His righteousness, and all these things shall be added to you."

19. **Before making any major purchase of a luxury item, wait!** Don't be in a hurry. Think! Is this what you want? Is it the only one available? Ask yourself, can you bargain further? Can you buy it elsewhere for less? Is the cost-per-use worth it? Eliminate impulse buying!

20. **Understand the law of compound interest.** Save $50.00 a month at 10%. In a year, you will have $600. In 25 years, you will have $66,000.

21. **Credit cards should be called convenience cards.** First, they charge interest, not give credit. Second, they tend to cause you to spend money you don't have. Pay with cash for purchases that do not need to be documented (like groceries, magazines, clothing). The less anyone else knows about what you do with your money, the better.

22. **If you want to buy a new car, recognize that the depreciation in the first year is horrendous.** So, consider a barely used or executive vehicle rather than a new one. Also, generally, the cheapest car is the one you own.

23. **Your checkbook shows where your heart is.** What you choose to spend your money on reflects what your priorities are.

24. **One more time to make sure you get this gem of wisdom from Bill Curry, "As you go through life, you will either pay the pain of discipline now, or you will pay the pain of regret later."**

To summarize what the Scriptures say about finances, David Jeremiah suggests we be wary of debt, restrain spending, save prudently, invest wisely, and give generously!

Readers Digest had a story about a hapless couple who were poor money managers. The man said to his wife, "The bad news is we owe $100,000 in college loans for the kids, a month's salary in back taxes, and our retirement fund is tanking." The wife asked, "Is there any good news?" The husband replied, "Yes! Our identity has been stolen!"

Buying habits have changed with the advent and rapid expansion of easy credit, low-interest rates, and the development of a credit card economy. There used to be just two classes of people: the rich-haves and the poor-have-nots. Now we have a third- the charge-its! Bits and Pieces told of an oxymoron sign in the window of a loan office that would have instant appeal to that latter group. Some lenders and credit card companies advertise, "Now you can borrow enough money to get completely out of debt!"

And then there is what is described by many as the most significant financial and mathematical discovery of all time, I say one more time, which is the principle of compound interest. For example, if one started, at age 22, to put $2,000 every year into an IRA or with a wealth management firm, which invests with discretion for you, the growth would have outstripped inflation over the years. As a result, your modest investment would be worth hundreds of thousands of dollars by retirement time of age 65!

Many among the elderly only wish to have enough money to live out their lifetime in reasonable comfort. Golfer Doug Sanders humorously put it this way, "I'm working as hard as I can to get my life and my cash to run out at the same time. If I can just die after lunch next Tuesday, everything will work out perfectly."

Here's another story from *Bits and Pieces*. An American Indian came into a bank to borrow $5,000. The bank manager asked for collateral. The American Indian wanted to know what that was.

The manager explained, "That is something of yours that has a value that we hold in exchange for the money you borrow."

The American Indian said, "Have five horses." The manager said OK.

The American Indian brought in his horses and walked out with the money. He came in the next week with a check for $100,000 and paid off the loan.

The manager is interested in gaining another depositor for the bank and suggested, "Why don't you leave some of the rest of that money with us on deposit?"

To which the American Indian replied, "How many horses you got?"

Will Rogers, a humorist in the 1920s and '30s said, "There was a time when a fool and his money were soon parted, but now it seems to happen to everybody." Still valid 100 years later in 2022.

Once again, for the third time, "the difference between the wealthy and the poor is the way they think." (I intentionally repeat some of these nuggets of wisdom to make sure you get them). Write it down. In a nutshell example, poor people think short term, whereas the wealthy understand delayed gratification and think long term. Both T. Harv Eker in his book Secrets of the Millionaire Mind: Mastering the Game of Wealth and Robert Kiyosaki in The Cash Flow Quadrant espouse the concept that rich people are often paid based upon results, whereas poor people get paid based on time. You'll never get rich working for somebody else.

Finally, being poor is a state of mind. Being broke is a temporary condition you can fix.

Choosing to Make a Wise Use of Time

Time is the one ingredient that has been equally distributed to all of us. We all get 24 hours in a day and seven days in a week. Time is our constant companion on our sojourn through life, which reminds us to use it wisely, for its segments are soon gone and not to be retrieved. We can lose and regain property, friends, money, and even opportunity, but time that is gone is just that — gone! It is the only commodity that cannot be recovered. Thus, what we do with the time we are given is one of the most essential other choices. If it is used constructively, one advances in life. If not, one declines. It is that simple!

Rudyard Kipling, in the closing lines excerpted from his inspirational poem "If," says it all.

> *If you can fill the unforgiving minute*
> *With sixty seconds' worth of distance run,*

> *Yours is the Earth and everything that's in it,*
> *And - which is more - you'll be a man, my son!"*

True happiness really does mean having a full calendar. Busy people get more done and are generally happier. But, as the well-known proverb states, "An idle mind is the devil's playground." The mind can get you into trouble with not enough to do.

During those frenzied years of accomplishment, when Molly and I were sleeping fast and running hard, we started a routine to help us overcome the tiredness we felt when it was time to rise and shine. Whoever was up first would shout enthusiastically, "Another day in which to excel!" But, of course, such a joyous greeting was not always matched by an equally positive response. Still, it helped us overcome our lethargy and begin the day.

We didn't know it then, but there was a biblical basis for our morning routine. We learned later that the Bible suggests that enthusiasm is the proper way to greet and start each day. From the book of Ruth 2:4, we learned how Boaz went into the fields to greet the harvesters by shouting: "The Lord be with you!" The workers responded by shouting back, "The Lord bless you!" Another scripture fit perfectly with what we were doing each morning. From Psalm 118:24,

> *This is the day the Lord has made; we will rejoice*
> *and be glad in it.*

I know a man in the prime of his life who, because he has a job and faithfully works Monday through Friday, feels he is entitled to sleep in on both Saturday and Sunday mornings. This has gone on for years. How much productive time has been lost? During our healthy, productive years, 5 to 6 hours of sleep is adequate. Additional time sleeping, while pleasurable, is not necessary! Just to make sure, one last time, from Bill Curry, "As you go through life, you must either pay the pain of discipline now, or you will pay the pain of regret later." If you get nothing more from reading this book, I'll be disappointed, but if you at least get that nugget of wisdom, your time has not been wasted.

The clock is always running. Time marches on. What you do with the time you are given is your decision. Only you can choose how it is spent. The two most frequently given excuses for any request are: I don't have the time and/or I don't have the money. We have learned that this thinking is false logic because everyone finds the time and money to do what they deem essential. Therefore, choices become a matter of priorities! Some learn that there is no such thing as FINDING time. We must conscientiously MAKE time available to invest it.

Perhaps the most compelling questions of priorities are these two. What if you were told you only had twenty-four hours to live? How would you spend the time? These extreme questions illuminate the pattern we already know about our habits. Not just for procrastinators but for most people, the "last minute" is and has always been THE MOST PRODUCTIVE PERIOD OF TIME IN THE HISTORY OF MANKIND. It is not likely that any of us will ever be asked those questions in all seriousness. It might be nice to have a warning of death, but that would also cause great consternation. Maybe nature's plan of surprise is better.

Take the story of the patient who went to his doctor to get the results of his medical tests. The Doctor said, "I've got some bad news and some worse news for you. The bad news is that the tests show that you only have twenty-four hours to live."

"Oh, wow! That's terrible." said the anguished patient. "What could possibly be the worse news?"

The Doctor replied, "I tried to reach you yesterday!"

For many people, sleeping takes up the most significant percentage of time in their lifetime. It is disproportionately high for the person sleeping in on Saturday and Sunday morning. A 40-hour or more workweek for twenty, thirty, or forty years takes up the next largest block of time for most. This leads us to consider the matter of "spare time." This term is somewhat of an oxymoron because it is basically a leftover on the hands of the clock and raises the question, what to do with it? There are two schools of thought on the matter: The first is procrastination, putting off doing, and giving priority to play. The second is giving work priority, focusing on productivity, accomplishment, and advancement.

From my perspective at age 92 looking at life, the conclusion I draw is that for each person, their choice goes back to what kind of a life they want as to how they spend their time. To make the most of our talents and serve other people, we must engage fully in the second choice, at least for our most productive years up to at least age fifty or sixty. At the same time, you have the energy, good health, and maximum motivation to accomplish your goals. All three of those human qualities diminish with age. Suppose a person does not make the most of what one has during the productive years. In that case, they are liable to come up short, at the far end of life, as too many eventually find out too late.

The end of life is always a surprise and tends to sneak

up on you. After all, life is like a roll of toilet paper; the closer you get to the end, the faster it goes! When anyone asks me, "How is it being 92?" My standard answer has become, "It's like the guy who fell out of a 50-story building. He was heard to say as he passed the 10th floor, 'So far, so good!'"

A friend had these words on a plaque over his office door.
This is the beginning of a new day.
What I do today is important.
Because I'm exchanging a new day of my life for it.
When tomorrow comes, this day will be gone forever,
Leaving in its place, whatever I traded for it.
I pledge that it shall be for gain, good, and success.
In order that I shall not regret the price I paid for this day.

As we go through life, everyone will experience good times and bad. Dexter Yager always maintained that it is not what happens to you through good times or bad, but, rather, how you handle it. Renowned pastor Robert Schuller of the Crystal Cathedral famously said, "Tough times don't last. Tough people do!"

The following analogy is given in the book, *Leadership When the Heat's On* by Danny Cox and John Hoover.

If you had a bank that credited your account each morning with $86,400, carried over no balance from day to day, allowing you to keep no cash in your account, canceling all unused funds at the end of each day, what would you do? Well, you have such a bank. It is called time. Every morning, each person's account is credited with 86,400 seconds. Every night, it is canceled. Time carries no balance forward. Nor does time allow us to borrow allocations against the future. We can only live on today's deposit and invest our time toward the maximum health, happiness, and success.

I might add, lost time is never found again!

I end this segment on the choice of using time with a quotation from long gone clergyman Henry Van Dyke:

> *Time is*
> *Too slow for those who wait*
> *Too Swift for those who Fear,*
> *Too Long for those who Grieve,*
> *Too Short for those who Rejoice,*
> *But for those who love*
> *Time is not.*

Choosing a Place to Live

Seeds grow where planted. An acorn does not fall far from the tree. What follows is a true story. When I was in high school, my parents took me on a trip down Skyline Drive and the Blue Ridge Parkway through Virginia and North Carolina. We stopped at one of the scenic overlooks looking down into a secluded valley. There was a log cabin and a small farm below. As we watched, a farmer was hitching up his horse to do the plowing. We didn't see any roads leading in or out of the valley.

As loud as I could, I called down to the farmer in curiosity, "We don't see a road. How did you get there?"

The farmer looked up and replied, "Born here!"

I asked, "Have you lived there all your life?"

His reply came back, "Not yet!"

There has been greater population mobility since World War II. We are no longer confined to a limited geographic area by a valley (like the farmer in my story), family tradition, or lack of means. Mass transit, air transportation, and interstate highways have erased barriers to travel. A person can decide to live anywhere. Frequently a job assignment or opportunity may dictate a geographic move. Also, today with the advent of computer technology, the opportunity to "work at home" has expanded dramatically and with it the possibility to live elsewhere rather than near the office. It is now possible to live at one location and be employed in an entirely different state. This has further enhanced mobility.

Last night, while channel hopping, I came across a program that went on for several hours featuring various couples moving to Montana. It showed them looking at several homes before choosing to purchase one in which to live. It created the impression that many people were leaving a variety of other cities and states and moving to scattered towns all over Montana, the "Big Sky" country. I must say it looked appealing. Beautiful scenery of wide-open spaces, mountains, meadows, lakes, and streams suggested wholesome outdoor living, recreation, and freedom.

In the established pattern, many people still commute in and out of a city, back and forth, between work and home life in the suburbs or country. However, in recent years because of increased crime, higher taxes, faulty city leadership, and over-regulation, people are fleeing big cities, even fleeing states with objectionable, oppressive, and intrusive patterns. The "work at home" possibilities have contributed to the exodus.

We have come a long way from the dependency on the mill village and the company store. With increased freedom and mobility, you can live anywhere. Why not? Just pick a place. Magazine articles, e-mails, and websites pop up constantly, like "Best Small Cities in America to Live"" Today I received an e-mail entitled "The Worst Towns in Each State."

There is plenty of information available to help you decide.

I recently heard a political commentator strongly suggest that we should live in an area of like-minded people. But unfortunately, with each passing year, our nation seems to become more polarized in our thinking, politics, and spirituality. During WWII, we were at our most unified and dominant point in history. Since then, we have been sliding down and today are a nation weakened and very divided. But more about that in the next segment on political choices.

I mention the community of like-minded people suggestion because it presents an interesting concept that is very timely considering the degree of civil unrest, increased crime, and intrusive city, state, and federal policies we have seen in recent years. Migration has begun by businesses and individuals seeking relief or improvement in another location, from blue cities and states to red ones. The problem then becomes sometimes the very problems that led to their migration, too often they bring with them. Then, without changing their thinking, they turn around, reconstitute and support, in their new location, the very same kind of events, politicians, and policies that caused them to leave in the first place! They don't seem to understand cause and effect.

Once again, it comes back to choosing based on one's principles, goals, and what kind of a life you want to live. I have watched the TV program "Life Below Zero" about the free lifestyle of those choosing to live near the Arctic circle. That certainly is not for everyone. Only the tough survive. But those who do, enjoy greater freedom and don't have the government breathing down their neck. As a matter of fact, that location is chosen by very few. Few people in vast lands, no conveniences, and harsh weather are the antithesis of big-city dwellings in the lower states.

Still, where you decide to live is one of the other significant choices of your life and will impact several of the other choices.

Choosing Your Nation

As I have stated before, this book is written by a patriot from a conservative and Christian perspective. I cannot compromise on this as these principles form my core convictions. In attempting to give you, the reader, ideas to contemplate regarding choosing your nation, I want to stick to the facts, point out the dichotomy of choices you face, and ask relevant questions ala the Socrates' method to cause you to choose one direction or the other.

Once again, your choices boil down to three. First, you can do nothing, opting not to take a position at all. However, as Plato cautioned,

> *If you do not take an interest in the affairs of your government, then you are doomed to live under the rule of fools.*

Secondly, you can align yourself with the left, which in our current political climate seems to be leading to socialism. I would caution that socialism throughout history has never worked anywhere and only leads to the misery of the people. Your third option is to the right, following the conservative, Christian principles upon which this country was founded, thus creating the greatest nation in the world.

There is no compromise in these choices, no in-between, no safe, satisfactory, or wise middle ground. It is an either-or choice at this point before it is too late! We are standing the edge of a precipice! As a nation, we are in danger of sliding down the slippery slope into socialism. I'm sure you can discern where I stand on the issues, but which position you take is yours to choose. Our nation is divided and poised at a fork in the road. Examine the issues carefully and choose wisely. The future direction of our nation is at stake.

Since the discovery of the Western Hemisphere and particularly upon the founding of our republic, we have drawn immigrants from the rest of the world. People were attracted to our shores and have chosen to come to our nation based on what is has represented in its history, the land of the free and the home of the brave. One can judge a country's freedom by whether people want to come to it or whether they want to flee from it. In choosing a country, it takes a thimble full of common sense to determine that you would seek the country that is drawing people to it, for it has broad appeal. Some came here to escape persecution. Some came simply to seek greater opportunity and hopefully have a better way of life. This continues today.

It is no secret that our founders were predominately Christians, acknowledged God, and adhered to the Judeo-Christian ethic as a philosophical foundation for our governance. On dozens of our government buildings in Washington, DC, the name of God is engraved in stone, assuring His place of prominence. These Christian ideals are reflected in our founding documents, the Declaration of Independence, the Constitution, and our Bill of Rights. Only since World War II have we, as a nation, turned our back on God.

Unfortunately, too many of our current politicians are

neither religious nor morally ethical. It was our second President, John Adams who said, "Our constitution was made only for a moral and religious people. It is wholly inadequate for any other." His insight implies the underlying fabric and dominance of traditional morals and conservative Christian ethics. This then evokes a firm foundation of absolute standards rather than a sliding moral scale of application based on current societal patterns, whatever they may be.

QUESTION: Would you choose these same principles to still guide our nation?

What a unique opportunity our founding fathers had. They chose to form a new nation unlike any other in the history of mankind. It was to be a land of the people, by the people, and for the people. Not a country ruled by a king or small group of elitists with unlimited power over the masses. History has taught us that absolute power corrupts absolutely! The story has been often told that, at the conclusion of those historic days in Philadelphia formulating the constitution, someone shouted out to Ben Franklin, "What have we got? A republic or a monarchy?" To which Franklin replied, "A republic. If you can keep it." That founding provided the framework which enabled the United States of America to become the greatest country in the world.

The QUESTION we face today for our nation is: Would you choose to follow the successful pattern established by our founding fathers or pursue a pattern of socialism that has only brought misery to its citizens and has never worked successfully anywhere?

Politically, I have always thought of myself as a sort of middle of the road kind of guy, that I could see both sides of the street, the left and the right. However, over my lifetime, I have observed that the road in America is not straight. It changes. During the 20th century, it was gradually drifting to the left. Then a few years back it took a sharper turn to the left. Ever zig-zagging, it veered back somewhat to the right for a while. Then more recently the focus has taken an even more severe turn to the left with the radical liberal socialist fringe having wrested control of government. The result of which is that I end up further to the right, respectively. I have not changed my position but appear to have shifted relatively. I have not changed my beliefs, but certainly have become firmer in my convictions.

Another example of this gradual transition to the left can be seen in the policies of one of our esteemed presidents. Going back to the early sixties, President John F. Kennedy was a Democrat and considered a liberal at that time. He has been revered by the mainstream press to this day. However, he was a patriot who loved, fought for, and served his country. His policies—particularly regarding tax cuts, foreign policy, and gun rights — considered liberal back then, would now be thought of as conservative, the road has shifted left to that degree. Today, instead of being revered, Kennedy would likely be maligned by the mainstream media, as are all current conservatives.

To be perfectly clear, again, this book is written by a patriot from a conservative, Christian perspective. Mine is the same perspective demonstrated by the founders of our country in 1776 as they were predominately Christians, conservatives and unquestionably patriots! It is also the same perspective held by the two founders, Jay VanAndel and Rich DeVos, of one of America's most successful corporate examples of free enterprise and entrepreneurship, Amway (a contraction of two words, American way). Both Rich and Jay made no bones about holding those same values. Rich DeVos stated at the 50th anniversary celebration of the founding of the company in Las Vegas said, "Our Christian values have provided the pattern for our corporate direction since its founding." My mentor Dexter Yager has said, "When you know what socialists stand for, what they propose, and what their agenda is, you cannot be for both socialism and for free enterprise. The two concepts are totally incompatible!"

Taking a position, as I have done being a Christian, conservative, patriot, and having traditional values, does two things:

1 – It matches the foundational concepts of our nation and parallels the pillars of the Amway Corporation which are freedom, family, hope and reward.

2 – It alienates those not open to a Biblical based worldview. I believe such a closed-minded attitude has become, "don't confuse me with the facts, my mind is made up." Their intolerance is based on man's judgment. Too bad. We as Christians are adamant as well, but instead, our opinions are based upon God's judgment. A guiding light for me in writing this book was to align, in principle, each of the choices discussed with God's word. There can be no other standard!

In the Bill of Rights, we are guaranteed certain freedoms. In his endearing painting by artist Norman Rockwell, he depicted four national ideals: freedom of speech, freedom of religion, freedom from want, and freedom from fear. Instead of instilling traditional pride in our history, there has been a recent emergence of a movement that would take us in a totally different direction. There are divisive evil forces in our nation. Following this mindset are those who instead of edifying our heroes of history, tear down their statues and malign them. These people seem to have exercised a growing influence to curtail free speech, to stamp out any opposing opinions, to criticize any who offer up conflicting ideas, to spin and manage the truth.

There is an element in our midst, who seek to stamp out opposition and free speech, to have a BIG, consuming, all powerful centralized socialist government run by elitists, leading to a one-party system. This direction runs counter to our founding, tradition, and operation for over 200 years. Ronald Reagan maintained that instead of BIG government, the best government was the LEAST government, for it is less intrusive in the lives of the people. Without naming political parties, I would suggest that everyone should examine the party platforms and proposals of each party and then vote for those whose party ideals most closely match Christian Biblical teachings.

QUESTION: Which is the direction would you choose for your country?

Our choice of direction has seldom confronted greater disparity. Our country has become polarized to a greater degree than ever before, except perhaps during the Civil War. Then it was the North—South difference over slavery, economics, and states' rights rather than the left liberal—right conservative differences found today. There is minimal common middle ground today. Instead, we have conflicting ideologies, disagreement, grid lock, stalemates, animosity, and partisanship.

Furthermore, with extreme partisanship now dictating party policy, we no longer see an overriding desire, on the part of many of those elected to serve, to do the right thing for the American people. Too often, politicians give only lip service to the citizenry. It is difficult to believe what some politicians say, when their actions become so different from their words. What they say and do simply don't match up. Their words often are nothing but schmooze. What we are getting from many politicians is spin and unfulfilled promises. It has been reported that the opinion and approval ratings of politicians have sunk to the lowest level in many years.

The dominant aim now for many politicians is the consolidation of party power, promising anything to win re-election, maintaining a place of permanence in Washington, eliminating any opposition, cheating and lying when necessary. This socialist pattern has never worked in any country where it has been tried. Churchill said, "Socialism is the philosophy of failure, the creed of ignorance, and the gospel of envy." He also said, "The main vice of capitalism is the uneven distribution of prosperity. The main vice of socialism is the even distribution of misery!" We face a choice for the future of our country.

QUESTION: Which future for our nation do you choose?

Some politicians today in Washington are attempting to skirt around the Constitution, even violating their oath to uphold, protect and defend it. Some are willing to attempt to manipulate the electoral process to result in a one-party socialist system, with an elite ruling class.... them! They strive to eliminate any opposition. There have been numerous recent examples of the application of overwhelming, vindictive force used by federal powers to crush and humiliate those in opposition. They even propose to "pack" the Supreme Court with additional liberal, activist judges who want to re- interpret the constitution by manipulating the laws. After all, the law has become what the court says it is, the ultimate authority. Today we have unelected judges skirting the Constitution, by making policy, and reinterpreting laws. The founding fathers wanted the Judicial branch to be the least dominant of the three branches, not the final authority it has become today.

QUESTION: Is this the nation you choose?

Furthermore, many immigrants originally came to our shores to be free from intrusive, oppressive, draconian government policies in their lives. They applied courage, individual initiatives, and a strong work ethic to conquer this wild, rough, hostile, untamed land, overcoming hardships to build the greatest country the world has ever seen. Immigrants came to contribute to society rather than the handout-oriented attitude of the illegal, undocumented immigrants streaming in masses through our borders today. Amazingly, they are even being welcomed and encouraged to come in the thousands by our government. They then become wards of the state, the beneficiaries of someone else's tax dollar. When a country institutes a policy of taking from the producers to give to the non-producer, its days are numbered indeed. We have created a society of takers! A wise man once said, "A nation without borders is no nation at all." We must also consider that without one official, dominant language, further division will exist among its people.

QUESTION: Is this the nation you choose?

An 18th century historian, Alexander Tyler, from Scotland,

forecast the following process which has been escalating in the USA in recent years. Consider the sequential results of such policies in determining your choice for direction of our nation! Simple cause and effect.

> *A democracy cannot exist as a permanent form of government. It can only exist until the voters discover that they can vote themselves largesse out of the public treasury. From that moment on, the majority always votes for the candidates promising the most benefits from the public treasury, with the result that a democracy always collapses over loose fiscal policy followed by dictatorship. The average age of the world's great civilizations has been 200 years. These nations have progressed through this sequence: From bondage to spiritual faith; From spiritual faith to great courage; From great courage to liberty; From liberty to abundance; From abundance to selfishness; From selfishness to apathy; From apathy to dependence; From dependence back into bondage.*

QUESTION: Is this the destiny you would choose for our nation?

A wise man once said, "Those who don't understand history are destined to repeat it!" Wake up, America!

I'd like to briefly revisit *Chapter Two, Choosing Your Mate*, to enunciate once more the following idea. When in the romantic hunt for a mate, do not, "for a skinny minute," ignore discussions of politics and religion. These are two subjects which sooner or later will require agreement or marital difficulties will ensue. Likewise, once one is a believer and has chosen your Lord, you have already taken a political position upon which to stand. There can be no compromise on principle.

Compare the platform of the two parties and see which

comes closest to the teachings of Scripture. To do so, makes a choice of voting on principle very simple and clear. According to Dennis Delisle, in his book *Calling the Called*,

> *Today it looks like somewhere between 5% and 20% of the people in the United States are moving America away from Godly principles to secularism. The 80% to 95% can't remain uninvolved and un-educated anymore, if we are to save the principles the Founders established for our country.*

Too many Americans vote based on a candidate's appearance, personality, or phony promises. We need term limits so that politicians don't become ensconced in Washington. That was never the intention of our founding fathers. Most of the current crop of legislators go to Washington with good intent, as average citizens, only to be corrupted by the system, and retire decades later as millionaires, by feathering their own nest. A career in government was never originally conceived as a pathway to wealth. In government, promises don't last, policies do.

One of my favorites sayings is, "If you are not a liberal at age 25 you have no heart. If you are not a conservative at age 35, you have no brain."

CHAPTER SEVEN

Conclusion

As I began to write the conclusion, the giant ball descended on Times Square, marking the official ending of 2021 and the beginning of the New Year, 2022. And yes, I have celebrated that another year has gone by without having had to use algebra (actually since eleventh grade in 1945-46). Of course, the ending of the calendar year means more than a celebration of that.

Another year has slipped into the history books. This provides us with the opportunity for a thoughtful time to reflect on the course of our lives. Have the choices that you have made so far in life brought you to where you want to be? It is an excellent time to take an assessment of your progress. Will continuing to do the same things you are currently doing bring the results you want? Should you expect that doing the same thing will get DIFFERENT or BETTER results?

When I was 42, I realized that if I continued on the same path for another year, I would simply be a year older, not necessarily better off. Also, that in twenty more years, I would become like the tenured professors ahead of me, who looked tired, wore sports coats with patches on the elbows, drove ten-year-old cars, and were mired in university politics. It was then I concluded that with four children, two BIG dogs (a Great Dane and a St. Bernard), and a rundown house to fix up, living from paycheck to paycheck every two weeks wasn't going to get us where I wanted to go. I needed to either do

151

something more or something different if I was to have the lifestyle I dreamed about.

You should start each new year with honest introspection, seeking mentorship, and asking the Lord for direction, prayerfully seeking His will in your life. Whatever you and the Lord agree to cannot fail. "Seek ye first the kingdom of God and His righteousness; and all these things shall be added unto you" Matthew 6:33.

What next? Where do I go from here, you ask? Need I be doing more? Should I be doing something different? In his "Finishing Well" message, David Jeremiah writes that Paul told the Ephesians that nothing mattered to him except finishing the work and the race the Lord had given him. Jeremiah then asks, "If someone were to record your story, would you have the same attitude as Paul?" That is an attitude of commitment to what you are doing! Would you have the same dedication, pursuit, and confidence that you are on the right path for yourself?

Answers to those questions involve important choices in at least some of the areas discussed earlier in this book. Life is short. It goes by in a hurry, faster than you think, more quickly than you expect. And faster than you want! Time marches on. It waits for no one. At 92, I speak from the authority of personal experience. I no longer feel invincible. However, I do feel immortal....so far.

My conclusion is that choices are intertwined with your life itself! As said in chapter one, setting aside heredity and environment, you are where you are in life because of the cumulative results of your choices. As Mike Huckabee once said, "For all of us life began 'once upon a time.' Unlike the fairy tales, however, it's up to us to make choices that determine whether the last line of our life stories will read, 'And they lived happily ever after.'"

Having told you about my three near-death experiences, I ponder the possibility that, by stretching my imagination, just a little bit, maybe, the Lord may have kept me alive just long enough to write, finish, and publish this book. If so, I have now finished. If that be the case, Lord, please keep in mind that, while I look forward to being with You in heaven, I am not in a hurry to get there.

However, should I suddenly be taken home, now that I have finished, it would lend some credence to the idea that He wanted me to write and finish this book first. In other words, He thought it was essential to be done. Now, how about that! What could be better than an endorsement from The Almighty? If so, this book would close the final chapter of my life, my last contribution that may hopefully have influence beyond my days. Mike Huckabee suggested we should "plant the seeds in this life which will yield fruit forever. We must choose to live beyond our lifetime." We must strive to have a lingering influence beyond our days, a legacy to benefit others.

In his daily devotional entitled "Keep Looking Forward," Pastor Ed Young wrote,

> *Thank God for your past achievements, and ask Him to prepare you to press on and focus on what is ahead. I guarantee that, in Christ, the best is yet to be!*

I get that same message as I read David Jeremiah's book *Forward*. Let me paraphrase some opening thoughts from his book. He reminds us that all of our experiences in life so far have prepared us for what we will face going forward. We should not fear the future. We should use our future to advance God's kingdom. He wants us to be optimistic and believe that the best is yet to come. Jeremiah put it this way, "When you first seek the kingdom of God and His righteousness, your future is always unfolding at the speed of grace."

Perhaps, my book may — instead of being a closing door, a final statement, or some parting thoughts — open a new door for me, of opportunity and service, a new path to walk, another assignment to pursue to follow His will. Maybe for you too, dear reader, another challenge, another choice. Who knows? I don't know. But He knows!

> *May these words of my mouth and this meditation of my heart be pleasing in your sight, Lord, my Rock, and my Redeemer. (Psalms 19:14)*

Acknowledgments

I have subscribed to the publication Bits & Pieces for at least three decades. I have benefited from its many stories, quotations, inspiring examples of life, and wisdom contained therein. Thank you, Mr. Rob Gilbert.

My dear Aunt Sara subscribed to *Readers Digest* for at least 50 years and passed most of those issues on to me, which I treasured, saved, and perused over the years. Thank you, editors.

I want to thank those who took their time and brain-power to read my initial drafts and make suggestions:

Molly Hughes

Virginia and Ed Borkey

Doyle Yager

Rick Setzer

Ron Ball

Pastor Lynn Stewart

Sue Renard

Dr. George Bryniawski

Squire Rick Abrahams

About the Author

Dr. Roland Hughes grew up in suburban Philadelphia, earning his undergraduate degree ('51) from West Chester University, a Master's degree ('56), and a Doctorate ('68) at the University of Pennsylvania. Dr. Hughes completed post-doctoral studies at Arizona State and Temple Universities. He also taught at the University of Washington in Seattle and Temple University in Philadelphia. Roland poured into the lives of young people as a football, basketball, and baseball coach, a geography teacher, an assistant principal, a school administrator at one of America's top ten high schools, and a director of guidance. He closed out his educational career as an Associate Professor of Education at the University of SC in Columbia, having embarked on a very successful career as an entrepreneur.

Roland and his wife Molly developed a successful Amway business ('72 to present) that stretched across the USA and worldwide, from Hong Kong and Korea in Asia to Belgium and the Netherlands in Europe. The Hughes qualified as Diamonds for almost 40 years and grew many Diamonds in their organization. Roland and his wife Molly became Legacy Founders Diamond and charter members inducted into the Yager Group Hall of Fame.

The Hughes have four grown children, 13 grandchildren, and four great-grandchildren. They live in the foothills of South Carolina and have been successful in everything they have done in life, including their marriage of 63 years.

Made in the USA
Monee, IL
26 January 2024

52445255R00096